CONNECTING THE POSTCOLONIAL

Ngũgĩ and Anand

LINGARAJA GANDHI

ATLANTIC
PUBLISHERS & DISTRIBUTORS (P) LTD

ATLANTIC
PUBLISHERS & DISTRIBUTORS (P) LTD
7/22, Ansari Road, Darya Ganj, New Delhi
Tel.: +91-11-4077 5252, 2327 3880
E-mail: orders@atlanticbooks.com
Web: www.atlanticbooks.com

Reprint 2025

Published by Atlantic Publishers & Distributors (P) Ltd.

Printed & bound in India by Atlantic Print Services

This book is dedicated to my father
Late. C. Kale Gowda, a freedom fighter
and a Sarvodaya worker who infused
in me, even as a boy, passion for
the life of the mind

Acknowledgements

It was as a student of M.A., in 1982 that I conceived the subject of this book when I happened to study Ngugi's *Weep Not, Child.* I had infrequently dwelt on the subject for a decade till I finally took up this great task. I remember with deep sense of gratitude Prof. D.A. Shankar who helped me extensively in completing this book. I am greatly indebted to Prof. R. Ramachandra, my teacher who supervised my Ph.D. thesis with patience, and taught me with affection the value of patience in the pursuit of scholarship.

More than three years of correspondence and the interview with Dr. Mulk Raj Anand have been the great moments of my awakening. I cherish Anand's warmth, encouragement and concern shown in the period of the writing of the present book. It is also my privilege to record my indebtedness to Ngugi Wa Thiong'o who readily responded to my queries.

I have had the privilege of interaction with many foreign scholars, whom I met at Commonwealth Conference in Colombo in 1995. They include: Dr. Alastair Niven of England, Dr. Anna Rutherford, Dr. Cynthia Vanden Driesen and Marvin Gillman of Australia, Dr. Reimeinchneider of Germany, Prof. Ranjan Goonetilleke of Sri Lanka, Dr. Claudio and Isabella Maria Zoppi of Italy and Ezekial Alembi of Kenya. All of them evinced keen interest in my comparative study over the years. I thank them all.

I am indebted to my teachers—Dr. Damodar Rao, Prof. Anniah Gowda, Prof. Polanki Ramamurthy, Prof. U.R. Ananthamurthy, Prof. K.C. Belliappa and others who have been the sources of inspiration.

There are many others—colleagues and friends to whom I am happily obliged—Prof. B. Shivaraj, Prof. Anita Nester,

Prof. C. Naganna, Subba Rao, Prof. Hanur Krishnamurthy, Dr. Shyamala Ratnakar of Karnatak University, Prof. I.D. Tiwari of IKS University, Khairagarh, Shri C.K. Shivashankaramurthy and C.K. Rajalakshmi.

I must make a particular reference to my friend, Saketh Rajan, who met death, premature. Although, has no direct role to play in this book, it was he, who showed me as my classmate in B.A., in 1978, the path I am treading now, while he chose for himself a different path. I remember him with deep sense of affection. Also, three special people who left this earthly abode—Shri C.V. Keshavamurthy, Shri C.B. Siddiah and my father-in-law Shri J. Vishwanath—have left an indelible mark on my life without whose blessings I would not have been what I am. I record here my gratitude for their love and hospitality.

Special thanks are to my brothers-in-law Dr. Chandrashekhar, Consultant Anesthetist (UK), Dr. B.J. Sharath Chandra, Surgeon, and Mr. Narendranath, an Engineer in Software, Dr. Roopa Kamal (USA) and to Dr. K. Mahadev, Orthopaedic Surgeon, who have always supported me in my crucial hours of need.

I am beholden to my mother Siddamma, mother-in-law Nagamma and to my brothers C.K. Suryanarayana and C.K. Jayarame Gowda and to my wife Sowmya and children Navya and Nihal who eagerly awaited the arrival of this book.

My sincere thanks are to Sri A.P. Balaji who typed the script. I owe my thanks to Atlantic Publishers and Distributors for this eloquent production.

This long list of thanks-giving, perhaps, points only to the fact that my book, or better say any book, is a result not of any individual achievement but of the collective effort. Yet, inevitably this book has gone in my name. Apologies for my heroism; for my 'I'!

Lingaraja Gandhi

Preface

With Rabindranath Tagore winning the Nobel Prize for Literature in 1913, the literary centre started moving from its assumed location in the West to the rest of the world. That great Indian moment was, perhaps, the beginning of the growth and spread of literature, which is now being satisfactorily baptized 'Postcolonial Literature.' Various nomenclatures like Commonwealth Literature, New Literatures in English, World Literature Written in English, Non-Hegemonic Literature—employed to describe the body of writing emerging from former colonies are symptomatic of the problem involved in defining the postcolonial. It was Rushdie who described this new phenomenon in his four memorable words, 'the empire writes back,' which in Chinua Achebe's coinage becomes 'the empire fights back.'

Again, interestingly, the lead for moving of the political centre; dissolution of the empire and the granting of independence to the countries colonized by European powers came from India in 1947. The Indian liberation struggle led by Mahatma Gandhi became a unique example for the rest of the world to emulate, and most African countries attained Independence in 1960s. Thus, Tagore and Gandhi became symbols of freedom—literary and political—in the postcolonial world. In the present study, I have attempted to trace, particularly, the influence of Gandhi on Ngugi and Anand in their constructions of the fictional worlds. The influence, while it is quite evident on Mulk Raj Anand, Ngugi speaks of his introduction to the visions from non-European world when he was in Leeds where he studied commonwealth literature. And, Ngugi speaks of the importance of Gandhi as a symbol of anti-imperialist force in the interview given to me, which is appended to this book.

Through an exploration of literary and spiritual kinship between Mulk Raj Anand, a pioneer Indian English novelist and Ngugi wa Thiong'o (James Ngugi), a Kenyan novelist in exile, the present book seeks to understand the postcolonial and examines the central issues of the postcolonial world. Instead of applying some of the assumptions of the postcolonial theory to read the works of Anand and Ngugi, I have attempted to examine the language of the fiction each one employs in rendering the chosen fictional world. This is a first full-length comparative study of these two writers, and I have compared both writers side-by-side instead of in separated chapters.

Since each one's literary output is enormous and covers the genres, other than fiction, the present discussion is confined to Anand's *Untouchable, Coolie, Two Leaves and a Bud, The Village, Across the Black Waters, The Sword and the Sickle, The Road* and some short-stories and Ngugi's *The River Between, Weep Not, Child, A Grain of Wheat, Petals of Blood, Devil on the Cross, Matigari* and few short-stories. I have also taken into account the non-fictional writings of Anand and Ngugi since both have often said that their non-fictional writings are part of their imaginative writings.

Plot summation of the novels is generally avoided. Instead, I have highlighted some common components of Anand's and Ngugi's fictional worlds. For instance, (a) both writers have shown preference for adolescents as central characters in their works; (b) the type of consciousness that both writers attribute to their protagonists is not 'cerebral' but centered around the loins; (c) the attitudes of these two writers towards land, roads and towns in a colonial system are strikingly similar; the meanings of their lands are often rendered in terms of 'fig trees' unique to their lands—in the case of Anand it is the 'banyan' and 'pipal', and in Ngugi's works it is the 'mugumo' tree that becomes significant and (d) neither writers lets go an opportunity to make World Wars serve as an ingredient of their works.

Accordingly, the book contains the following sections: (1) Introduction, (2) Awakening, (3) The Excremental and the Genital, (4) Naked Land, (5) A Land Like All the Others and (6) Conclusion. I have also appended to the book the interviews with Ngugi and Anand, as well as Anand's letters. These letters and interviews permit a glimpse into the amazing concurrence that Anand and Ngugi display in their approaches to the problems of life and literature.

More than the language of fiction, or the eloquence of expression, it is the vision of each of these writers that has left a lasting impression on me. Their fictions visualize a society based on the human bond and equality. It would but be appropriate to conclude my preface with Ngugi's commitment for humanitarian vision of society well ingrained in his words: "We must all struggle for a world in which one's cleanliness is not depended on another's dirt, one's health on another's ill-health, and one's welfare on another's misery."

Lingaraja Gandhi

Contents

Introduction

1

Dissimilarities between Mulk Raj Anand and Ngugi Wa Thiong'o are self-evident. They belong to two distinct cultures: Indian and Kenyan. A generation separates the two contemporaries. Anand's career as novelist began with the publication of *Untouchable* in 1935, three years before Ngugi's birth. The latter's first novel, *Weep Not, Child* appeared in 1964. These differences though, are superficial; the points of contact between them are startling.

The greatest political reality for both is perhaps colonialism (in Ngugi's case, neo-colonialism as well). Their youthful days coincided with their nations' struggle for liberation from oppressive foreign rule; they grew up amidst turbulence. Born in 1905, Anand saw his country enter its intensest phase of the freedom movement when Gandhi returned from South Africa in 1915. Anand was arrested and caned by the police for innocently breaking the curfew during the Jallianwalla Bagh Massacre in 1919; in 1921 he was jailed for a brief period for participating in the Civil Disobedience Campaign against the British (Anand records these events in his autobiographical novels *Morning Face* and *Confession of a Lover*). "The era into which I was born," says Anand, "was... the turning point of my country" (*Apology for Heroism*, 71). That could as well apply to Ngugi. Ngugi was born in 1938 and grew up during the 'high noon' of colonial oppression and the native resistance; 1952-57 were the years of the Emergency and the Mau-Mau struggle in Kenya. He was deeply scarred during the Emergency, though he was not personally involved in the struggle. His brother Wallace Mwangi had joined the Mau-Mau after a dramatic escape from detention camp. His parents and relatives were put in detention. Understandably, young Ngugi became a suspect in the eyes of the homeguards. Painfully he recollects these and other details in his *Detained: A Writer's Prison Diary*. Returning from school after the first term in 1955, Ngugi was shocked to find his village reduced to ruins by the colonial forces:

> I came back after the first term and confidently walked back to my old village. My home was now only a pile of dry mudstones, bits of grain, charcoal and ashes. Nothing remained, not even crops, except for a lone pear tree that slightly swayed in sun and wind. I stood there bewildered. Not only my home, but the old village with its culture, its memories and its warmth had been razed to the ground (73-74).

Locating the new site to which the village had been shifted was no doubt a traumatic experience for the boy.

Experiences, which tormented them keep recurring in Anand and Ngugi. Images of 'police arrest,' 'lock-ups' and prison appear frequently in Anand's *Lalu Trilogy* and Ngugi's *Weep Not, Child, Petals of Blood, Devil on the Cross, Matigari* and *A Grain of Wheat.* The surprising similarity in their sensibility and moral outlook manifests in the manner they exploit the prison-image to describe the predicament of the native labourer in a colonized land. We may briefly compare the labourer Gangu in *Two Leaves and a Bud* and his counterpart Njoroge in "The Martyr" to see how the prison-condition of existence is fictionally enacted. In Anand's novel, Gangu from Punjab is enticed by Buta Ram to become a labourer in a tea estate in Assam. The irresistible temptation for Gangu is the promise of a strip of land. Arriving on the plantation early in the novel, the first thing Gangu sights is the lodging place. The English landlords appear to be proud of the brick huts they have constructed for their coolies. Gangu's wife is excited "at the sight of the little brick huts in the coolie lines covered with corrugated iron roofs" (*Two Leaves and a Bud*, 34). But Gangu knows that these brick and tin huts, when compared with his own mud hut, which he had built in his village, are ugly tin boxes that afford no shelter from heat, rain or wind. His suspicions are confirmed as he inspects the "dwelling" from inside:

> ... as Gangu entered the place behind his fluttering excited wife, he was confirmed in his misgivings, for the narrow little place, back to back with another hut presumably of the same size, was like a furnace with the heat radiated by the tin roof. He looked round the room, probing the corners where columns of darkness washed the light, and *he had a feeling of being closed in by the hard, impenetrable walls,* a feeling that he had never experienced surrounded by the soft clay of his village hut even when it was choked by smoke. And, at the same time, he felt like a towering pillar standing in the middle of the room (34-35) (Emphasis added).

This description evokes images of a prison. Gangu has to live in this cell with his wife and two children. The labourers' houses in "The Martyr" are no different from those of their counterparts in Anand's novel. Mrs. Hill thinks that she is extraordinarily generous and kind in getting rooms constructed for her labourers. Njoroge's thoughts and feelings however, are quite different. He offers us an inside view of their 'homes':

> He came to his own room. There was no smoke coming from all the other rooms belonging to the other workers. The lights had even gone out in many of them. ... It was a very small room. Sitting on the bed one could almost touch all the corners of the room if one stretched one's arms wide. Yet it was here, *here,* that he with two wives and a number of children had to live, had in fact lived for more than five years. So crammed! (*Secret Lives,* 44).

The predicament of a worker, as one can see from the passages, is no different from that of a prisoner. In both tales, the white settler is shown constricting the very space around the labourers who are but peasants disposessed of their ancestral land.

This parallel is enough to demonstrate the extent to which Anand's vision agrees with Ngugi. The plight of the meanest worker on the land offers the truest picture of colonialism.

The similarity is in evidence in their response to the schooling made available to them. Both went to English schools run by the British. Anand recollects that the education imparted in those schools was

> imitative, giving very little idea of Indian tradition, but mainly a bastardized version of English curricula, in English, with particular emphasis on English history, ideas, forms and institutions, deliberately calculated to show everything relating to Indian history and tradition as inferior... (*Apology for Heroism*, 12).

And so, Anand says, he acquired "a bias against all indigenous customs and grew up hating everything Indian" (*Apology for Heroism*, 12-13). Ngugi has the precise term to explain this kind of a child's upbringing: "Colonial alienation." The term means a "disassociation of sensibility of that child from his natural and social environment" (The Language of African Literature," *Decolonizing the Mind: The Politics of Language in African Literature*, 17). In sum, those were schools that taught the young natives to be servile to the English:

> So I grew up, like most of my contemporaries, a very superficial, ill-educated young man, without any bearings. My only ideal, if ideal it can be called, was one, which my father had accepted as a gift from the benign Sarkar—to pass all examinations and to secure a good subordinate job in the pay of the Government (*Apology for Heroism, 15*).

Ngugi initially went to a school run by nationalists, but since those schools were taken over by the colonial regime after the declaration of Emergency in 1952, he experienced drastic changes in the mode of education: "English became the language of my formal education: In Kenya, English became more than a language. It was the language, and all others had to bow before it in deference" (*Decolonizing the Mind*, 11). Ngugi recounts in *Decolonizing the Mind,* one of his humiliating experiences at school, where students dreaded being caught speaking Gikuyu:

> The culprit was given corporal punishment—three to five strokes of the cane on bare buttocks—or was made to carry a metal plate around the neck with inscriptions such as I AM STUPID or I AM A DONKEY ... how did the teachers catch the culprits? A button was initially given to one pupil who was supposed to hand it over to whoever was caught speaking his mother tongue. Whoever had the button at the end of the day would sing who had given it to him and the ensuing process would bring out all the culprits of the day. Thus children were turned into witch-hunters and in the process were being taught the ... value of being a traitor to one's immediate community (*Decolonizing the Mind*, 11).

Ngugi's career has a significant correspondence with Anand's, and that is his pursuit of education in England. Anand himself went to England in 1925, in order to escape from his prison-like condition in search of "personal freedom" (*Apology for Heroism*). In the case of both writers the intellectual climate of England contrasted sharply with that in their own educational institutions at home. In the Bloomsbury circle and in the "study circle of Marxist thought and practice" at the trade unionist Allen Hutt's, Anand came into contact with major novelists and radical thinkers like F.R. Leavis, Middleton Murry, Herbert Read, Stephen Spender, Aldous Huxley, D.H. Lawrence, Eric Gill and George Orwell. During his student's days in India, Anand could reach continental literature—especially Russian—through promiscuous reading, for none of the questions about the world, which he wanted to ask were answered. But England made it possible for him to interact with the best minds. That is also true of Ngugi who found the atmosphere in England free to allow questions. He kept meeting radical friends at discussions in Arnold Kettle's house and attended literary conferences in the United States, Moscow and Damascus. Accounts of their years abroad are available in their own writings, as well as in biographical sketches. What is of interest to a student of comparative literature is the sharp and penetrative insight with which these writers analyze the climate of Europe in their times. Anand emphasizes the greater validity of Asian and African (non-European) perspectives. In an essay, "Old Myth-New Myth: Recital Versus Novel," he observes:

> In the newly emergent agro-industrial civilizations of Asia and Africa, where the most revolutionary changes in history are taking place, the men and women of sensibility, though identified generally with libertarian aims, have entered the age of criticism, which seeks to relate the old myths to the new myths, to synthesize the inner spaces to the outer spaces (*Indian Literature of the Past Fifty Years,* 110).

He strongly sensed the beginning of new world-orders, which were not Eurocentric:

> Lenin and Nehru and Mao-Tse Tung, who have initiated the new techniques of the recently freed societies in our continent, have all sought to transform the 19th century mechanical Western concept of 'progress' into a dynamic, which they have variously called 'Dialectic', 'Discovery' or 'Cultural Revolution' (*Indian Literature of the Past Fifty Years,* 110).

It was as a novelist that Anand saw the emerging new models of the world: "A novel concerns the whole of human life" ("Old Myth-New Myth," 10). It was through the novel-form that Anand becomes aware of the changes of attitudes of his age. In a novel-infested world where it looks as if "every young man or young woman, particularly in the West, can and does write a novel or two in order to work off the hangover of an adolescent calf-love" (109), the need is to see the novel (by recognizing its limits) as a "weapon of humanism" (*Indian Literature of the Past Fifty Years,* 119).

Ngugi too saw clearly these new models. In his book *Moving the Centre*, he proudly announces that his *A Grain of Wheat* "symbolized a significant moment in the development of African Literature". That was the moment when

> the centre of the universe was moving from Europe or, to put it another way, when many countries particularly

> in Asia and Africa were demanding and asserting their right to define themselves and their relationship to the universe from their own centres in Africa and Asia (*Moving the Centre*, 2).

An indignant Ngugi asks:

> Were we to see the world through the European responses to imperialism of the likes of Rudyard Kipling, Joseph Conrad or Joyce Cary, whose work in terms of themes or location or attitude assumed the reality and experience of imperialism? (*Moving the Centre, 4*).

With illustrations, he asserts that if people were really to depend on European literature (even at its best), they could get a "very distorted picture of modern world, its evolution and its contemporary being." Hence his pride with regard to *A Grain of Wheat.* It "celebrated the more than sixty years of Kenyan peoples' struggle to claim their own space" (*Moving the Centre*, 3). It agreed with a new model of the world, which was Afro-centric and not Eurocentric.[1]

Anand's understanding of the global situation in the thirties increased his own political "responsibilities as a writer," though he did not need "lessons" in this respect for he says:

> ... in India life was politics and politics life, especially as most of us have grown up with some awareness of the method of the internment camp, of torture and prison and the suppression of civil and political liberties during the last quarter of a century (*Apology for Heroism*, 79).

Ngugi too stresses the political imperatives for the writer in his own age:

> The relationship between the poet and politician, or between writers and politics, is particularly important in our situation where our cultures, our literature, music, songs, dances—are developing under the strangulating embrace of western industrial and finance monopoly capital and the fierce struggles of our people for breath even (*Writers in Politics*, 72-73).

In the very process of articulating a people's collective consciousness, the writer is led into active political struggles.

Political awareness, it follows, means for Anand and Ngugi, awareness of human suffering, and they see this awareness unravelling itself in the struggle for non-European centres.

A liberal and global awareness is discernible in Anand and Ngugi, yet, the global becomes possible paradoxically, because of their fidelity to the 'local.' Such a relation between the 'local' and the 'universal' is expounded by Ngugi in his essay "The Universality of Local Knowledge" (*Moving the Centre*). His ambition as a writer is to see, in Blake's words, 'the world in a grain of sand':

> A novelist is almost wholly dependent on the particular. Whatever he may have to say about life, it must be rooted in the particularities of daily experience (*Moving the Centre*, 25).

There is nothing shallow about such local knowledge, he explains:

> Local knowledge is not an island into itself; it is part of the main, part of the sea. Its limits lie in the boundless universality of our creative potentiality as human beings (*Moving the Centre*, 25).

This is equally true to Anand's belief.

The chapters that follow attempt to understand the spiritual kinship of Anand and Ngugi mainly from this perspective. No effort is made to study the influence of one on the other; such an exercise does not promise much, for the two wrote independently of each other (as their letters in Appendix B indicate). This fact is easily grasped when we try to relate Fanon to their works. The same dialectics that one find in Fanon appears to operate behind these two great novelists. Yet, Anand was fairly advanced in his literary career much before the appearance of Fanon, and Ngugi who assiduously studied Fanon, began producing his works in the sixties, after Fanon's death.[2]

This thesis pays greater attention to their vision than to the fictional techniques they employ. Plot summation of the novels is generally avoided. Instead, some common components of their fictional worlds are highlighted. Both show a preference for adolescents as central characters in their works; their attitudes to land, towns and roads in a colonial system are strikingly similar; the meaning of their lands are rendered often in terms of fig trees unique to their lands; neither writers lets go an opportunity to make World Wars serve as an ingredient of his works.

Awakening (Chapter Two), through a discussion of the centrality accorded to young boys in the novels of Anand and Ngugi, elucidates the dilemmas of a society under colonial rule. The awakening of the national consciousness is seen in terms of the growth to maturity of adolescent boys like Bakha and Waiyaki. The yearning of an adolescent for adult status becomes an effective allegory of a nation's longing for independence. The young heroes are strategically placed at the threshold of adulthood to dramatize the conflict between the traditional and the modern. Since both natives and colonizers make urgent and mutually contrary demands on the very young (in accordance with the 'catch them young' policy), the chapter scrutinizes the manner in which mythification and demythification processes are made to operate behind both the colonizer and the colonized.

In both Ngugi and Anand, political, social and moral conflicts are rendered through a special evaluative consciousness—which is the theme of the third chapter, **The Excremental and the Genital.** In the fictional worlds of the two writers, it is not so much the adult intellectuals as the adolescents eagerly seeking full-membership of society who are instrumental in opening up the various shades of colonial conflict. Hence the importance of circumcision rites in Ngugi, and a preoccupation with the excretal function in Anand. It is through a consciousness centered around the waist—anal/genital consciousness—that the motivational tensions in the works of Anand and Ngugi are understood.

Since the two writers are intensely conscious of the agrarian character of their societies, the relationship between man and land acquires added significance. The fourth chapter, **Naked Land** analyzes the colonizer-colonized conflict in terms of the image of the land and the allusions to Scriptures. Ngugi alludes repeatedly to the Bible, especially the *Book of Exodus* and Anand to the *Mahabharata.* The complex inter-relatedness between the traditional and the modern is reflected in the image of the land. While land is the supreme index of power, might and dominance for the colonizer, for the colonized it symbolizes the past and all its associations—identity and dignity in particular. For the colonist, one land is perhaps not different from another, except in terms of the material produce it yields, but in a people who aspire for freedom, there exists a sense of uniqueness of their own land. The chapter analyzes how land that gets sacralized for the colonized is turned into a commodity by the colonizer.

Chapter five, **A Land Like All the Others** examines the way in which Anand and Ngugi bring out the poignancy in the predicament of the colonized, by depicting the colonizer-colonized clash on the colonizer's mainland, Europe. The chapter discusses references to the World Wars in the novels of Anand and Ngugi. Anand's *Across the Black Waters* has a First World War setting. There is no World War setting in Ngugi's novels, but the references to World Wars I and II in *Weep Not, Child, A Grain of Wheat* and *Petals of Blood* are suggestive enough to warrant a comparison. This section of the thesis also considers how the two writers bring out the utterly human need for land not only in a colonial, but in a broadly human context. What are the dramatic implications of the colonized people participating in a colonizer's war? Outside their territory, the colonized fight for the colonizer, while at home they fight against the colonizer—all this for the sake of their own land. The struggle for land continues even after political independence, because, people can understand 'freedom' only in terms of land. Land and freedom become important fictional constructs for Anand and Ngugi. The chapter discusses such a relationship.

The concluding chapter tries to establish the significance of the spiritual kinship between Anand and Ngugi and evaluates the achievements of their art and concerns. Writing in two culturally different yet similar political environments, Anand

and Ngugi have successfully recreated the experiences of their societies, which are affected by colonial cultures. The humanistic creed to which these two writers are committed lends a subtle moral dimension to their works.

The Interviews and Letters appended to the thesis permit a glimpse into the amazing concurrence that Anand and Ngugi display in their approaches to the problems of literature and life. To a query as to why young boys are made protagonists in their novels, Anand replies, "Because I saw in the young the future of India,"[3] and Ngugi answers, "The young embody the tomorrow of any community."[4] Straightforward and unambiguous answers. To another question as to why their protagonists are drawn from peasant stock, Ngugi says: "Peasant and worker. They are the most productive while being the most exploited in both colonial and post-colonial Kenya."[5] Compare this reply with Anand's: "I am fond of them. They are very vital people. They are genuinely human compared to the caste Hindus. The Sikhs are anti-castes."[6] That the caste-system is exploitative does not need elaboration. To another query as to why the novel is a major form for writers dealing with social and political issues, Ngugi comments: "The novel is essentially a continuation of the ancient story-telling traditions of most peoples in the world."[7] Anand's response is but an elaboration of the same point:

> All fiction, all writing except the *Shastras* (Canonical texts) are political in nature and have social purpose in mind. In *Mahabharat* one sees the model novel of the world. Without *Mahabharat* there is no Mulk Raj Anand or R.K. Narayan or Raja Rao. All our writing is in the tradition of *Mahabharat.* The Indian writer is writing *Mahabharat* all the time... The language of *Mahabharat* was the language of the time; no written language, but spoken, understood by the people.[8]

Hence it is "inevitable" that the novel should become the major form in Third World Literature.

Despite the striking similarities between Anand and Ngugi, comparative studies of these writers are not plentiful. In fact, at the time of the submission of this thesis, a single title—O.P. Mathur's "The Hero Between: A Study of Ngugi's Waiyaki and Anand's Lalu"—has found entry in the bibliography. A brief remark by P.K. Rajan about the possible likeness between Anand and Ngugi was reassuring.[9] Mathur's essay appeared in 1982 and Rajan's book in 1995; stimulus for this project came mainly from Jack Lindsay's observation that Anand was a "forerunner of the protest literatures of the colonial people as they threw off their oppressions" ("Mulk Raj Anand," *Kakatiya Journal of English Studies*, Spring 1977, 4).

What the present study hopes is to demonstrate that the nature of the literary kinship between Anand and Ngugi is such as to enable the elucidation of the works of one writer with the help of the other's.

Since the literary output of each of these writers is enormous and covers other genres than the novel and the short story, no attempt is made at a comprehensive study of all the available works of Anand and Ngugi. Discussions is limited to Anand's *Untouchable, Coolie, Two Leaves and a Bud, The Village, Across the Black Waters, The Sword and the Sickle, The Road* and some short stories, and Ngugi's *The River Between, Weep Not, Child, A Grain of Wheat, Petals of Blood, Devil on the Cross, Matigari* and *Secret Lives.*

NOTES

1. According to Feroza Jussawalla and Reed Way Dasenbrock to be "truly 'afro-centric,' one has to go back to writing in African languages, not writing in an European language such as English, and it has been the Kenyan writer Ngugi wa Thiong'o... who has carried this (by writing in Gikuyu) to the logical conclusion" (Introduction. *Interview with Writers of the Post-Colonial World.* By Feroza Jussawalla and Reed Way Dasenbrock. London: UP of Mississippi, 1992).
2. Anand's *Untouchable* and *Coolie* appeared in 1935 and 1936; the Lalu Trilogy was published before 1942. Fanon died in 1961. His famous book *The Wretched of the Earth,* appeared the same year. Ngugi's works were published 1962 onwards.
3. Appendix B, "An Interview with Dr. Mulk Raj Anand, p. 147.

4. Appendix A, "Interview with Professor Ngugi wa Thiong'o," p. 144.
5. Appendix A, "Interview with Professor Ngugi wa Thiong'o," p. 144.
6. Appendix B, "An Interview with Dr. Mulk Raj Anand," pp. 147.
7. Appendix A, "Interview with Professor Ngugi wa Thiong'o," p. 143.
8. Appendix B, "An Interview with Dr. Mulk Raj Anand," pp. 145-46.
9. "Protest literatures of the third world are all basically motivated by a revolutionary humanism; and the historical dialectic of the colonial situation that determines Anand's ambivalence seems to be a common feature of all of them. It therefore sounds logically possible that tendencies akin to Anand's are present in these writers, too, in varying forms and degrees. Ngugi wa Thiong'o of Kenya, for instance, is a writer who appears susceptible to this tendency" (*Mulk Raj Anand: A Revaluation*, 182).

WORKS CITED

Anand, Mulk Raj. *Apology for Heroism.* 1946. Bombay: Popular-Kutub, 1980.

Anand, Mulk Raj. *Confession of a Lover.* New Delhi: Arnold Publishers, 1976.

Anand, Mulk Raj. *Morning Face.* Bombay: Popular-Kutub, 1968.

Anand, Mulk Raj. "Old Myth-New Myth: Recital Versus Novel." *Indian Literature of the Past Fifty Years.* ed. C.D. Narasimhaiah. Mysore: U of Mysore, 1970.

Anand, Mulk Raj. *Two Leaves and a Bud.* 1937. New Delhi: Arnold Associates, 1994.

Lindsay, Jack. "Mulk Raj Anand." *Kakatiya Journal of English Studies. Mulk Raj Anand Special Number* 2.1, (1977) 4.

Rajan, P.K. *Mulk Raj Anand: A Revaluation.* New Delhi: Arnold Associates, 1995.

Thiong'o, Ngugi wa. *Decolonizing the Mind: The Politics of Language in African Literature.* 1986. London: James Currey, 1987.

Thiong'o, Ngugi wa. *Detained: A Writer's Prison Diary.* 1981. London: Heinemann, 1984.

Thiong'o, Ngugi wa. *Homecoming: Essays on African and Caribbean Literature, Culture and Politics.* 1972. London: Heinemann, 1982.

Thiong'o, Ngugi wa. *Moving the Centre: The Struggle for Cultural Freedoms.* London: James Currey, 1993.

Thiong'o, Ngugi wa. "The Martyr." *Secret Lives.* 1975. London: Heinemann, 1987.

Thiong'o, Ngugi wa. *The Writers in Politics.* London: Heinemann, 1982.

Awakening

2

Mulk Raj Anand and Ngugi wa Thiong'o (James Ngugi) favoured very young boys as central characters in many of their novels. The practice of making children and adolescents protagonists is neither new nor limited to novelists of any one culture. Dickens, Mark Twain, Kipling and Golding among many others have presented humanitarian viewpoints effectively through the eyes of children. But this book is interested in the portrayal of adolescents in colonial situations—such as those seen in *Untouchable, Coolie, The Village, The River Between* and *Weep Not, Child.*

The scope to encapsule in the state of adolescence the conflicts and contradictions of a society under colonial rule is immense. Adolescence provides a suitable arena to enact the clash of opposing cultures; an adolescent eagerly seeking the state of maturity offers excellent ground to contrapose the forces of tradition and the forces of modernity.

Doubts regarding the wisdom of granting centrality to adolescents have bothered some readers of Anand and Ngugi. Eustace Palmer, for example, is of the opinion that the

> ... main weakness of *Weep Not, Child* is the choice of Njoroge as the central consciousness. Not because Njoroge is too passive and ineffective to be at the centre of the novel's events, but because a young, inexperienced boy is not the best vehicle to demonstrate that an obsession with education as a panacea is escapist. It is in the nature of young boys to dream, and have illusions about the future, and one can hardly except them to understand the complexity of national affairs. The same

> tendency in an adult would have been much more convincing (*An Introduction to African Novel,* 10).

The generalization in Palmer's observation ("a young and inexperienced... escapist") appears to be incorrect. If a "young and inexperienced" boy like Huckleberry Finn serves to judge a whole civilization, why should young boys not be employed to present the "complexity of national affairs?"

With both Anand and Ngugi the choice of young protagonists for their works was quite deliberate. Ngugi considered young boys as specially responsive to a world that is in a state of transition. As Cook and Okenimpke observe:

> In a rapidly changing society like modern Kenya, it may be hard for older men to keep pace with the inexorable movements of history. Young men and women are needed, in key with the times, who are free from self interests and immune to the prejudices, both of power-magnates and of their own teachers (*Ngugi wa Thiong'o: An Exploration of His Writings,* 27).

Anand displays the same trust in youth when it comes to depicting reality. "The young cannot afford to stay neutral" (*Morning Face, 567*), he declares. One needs to remembers that these writers who found young boys particularly suited for centrality (in their works), were convinced that in a drastically changing system, it was impossible for one to stay neutral.

It may be relevant here to note Jean Paul Sartre's perceptive observation that the spread of colonial culture begins with the colonization of young boys—with the brainwashing of the young by Western values:

> The European *elite* undertook to manufacture a native *elite.* They picket out promising adolescents; they branded them, as with a red-hot iron, with the principles of western culture; they stuffed their mouths full with high sounding phrases, grand glutinous words that stuck to the teeth. After a short stay in the mother country they were went home, whitewashed (Preface, 7. *The Wretched of the Earth*).

The Headmasters of the Siriana Mission and representatives of Western ideology (in *Weep Not, Child* and *The River Between*) are examples of the European elite that Sartre mentions. The Headmaster in *Weep Not, Child* firmly believes in the supremacy of the white man's values and promptly imposes them on young boys. He brings up the schoolboys "to copy and cherish the white man's civilization as the only hope of mankind and especially of the black races" (115). In his mission of spreading Western culture and religion, Livingstone (in *The River Between*) too adopts the "catch-them-young" policy. He trains young natives like Waiyaki, Kamau and Kinuthia, and sends them to villages where they engage themselves in the mission of spreading European values. Livingstone "had always liked the idea of training some Mission boys who could be sent out to spread the good news"[1] (55). Joshua (caught young and trained in Siriana Mission) is one such early candidate who is "sent to spread the good news."

> He, along with a few others, had been the first to be converted to the new faith. He was then a young man who ran from the hills and went to live with the white man in the newly established Mission... The new faith worked in him till it came to possess him wholly. He renounced his tribe's magic, power and ritual (*The River Between*, 29).

This convert rejects the Gikuyu customs and practices with a vehemence not seen even in the white man (Livingstone). The native convert disowns his own daughters Muthoni and Nyambura the instant they either incline to Old Faith or old customs.

At the start of the colonization process, the young men, caught in Western euphoria, begin to doubt and even reject the indigenous values and ways of life. After returning from Siriana, Waiyaki (in *The River Between*) shows conspicuous changes in his attitudes, indicating the extent to which his mind is colonized by Livingstone's ideology. Earlier, whatever details regarding Gikuyu land and culture Chege had related to him were like 'visions;' but now he regards his father's ideas as an old man's illusions. Earlier, Waiyaki longed for circumcision, but after the Siriana trip he cannot participate in the circumcision dance and songs without embarrassment; he regards the whole ritual (including dance and songs, which according to Jomo Kenyatta are part of the initiate's education in tribal customs, traditions and beliefs)[2] as an act of 'tribal frenzy'—an expression that he has borrowed from Livingstone's ideology. One may recall a similar situation from Chinua Achebe's *Things Fall Apart*: Okonkwo's son Nwoye refuses to return to his father's ways once he is converted to Christianity. John Boy Junior in *Matigari* typifies a westernized native. The villagers send Boy, a poor native's son, to England for his higher studies. The natives fondly believe that John Boy, armed with the knowledge (power) of the white man, "shall come back and clean up our cities, our country and deliver us from slavery..." They see in John Boy "a future patriot." In other words, John Boy is expected to return with the brains of the colonizer and the heart of a patriotic native. But contrary to the natives' hopes John Boy's education in England sees him fulfill the colonizer's design of manufacturing westernized natives who serve as the settler's parasite. On his return, the natives discover that Boy has forgotten the people who supported him and has lost all respect for their ways, customs and language. He contemptuously remarks: "But you black people? You walk about fettered to your families, clans, nationalities, people, masses" (49). Such figures, 'black elites' are to be seen even in *A Grain of Wheat* (62).

Since colonization begins with the adolescents, it is natural to expect of decolonization too to begin with the young. In *The River Between* Waiyaki's father Chege, considered a representative of native ideology, is nagged by a sense of failure to awaken his people against the white man's invasion of the Gikuyu land. But it is his belief that his son, because he is young, has the ability to resist alien ideology. And so he entrusts to Waiyaki the responsibility of maintaining the unity and purity of the tribe. Chege was opposed to the Siriana Mission (*i.e.*, Livingstone's ideology) all through his life. Yet he sends his son to the very place, in the hope that it would equip him better in the struggle against colonial occupation of the Gikuyu land. Kabonyi too, who represents the orthodox native culture sends his son to Siriana. He too believes that his young son Kamau needs to be trained in the white man's ways in order to fight him.

In a world where "de-colonization" has advanced significantly, the "European elite" becomes transparent to his own irrelevance in the native's land. *Untouchable* is a work where the nationalist movement is shown approaching its peak. Natives in *Untouchable* readily recognize the irrelevance of a missionary like Colonel Hutchinson of the Salvation Army. The attitude of every native to this missionary is marked by a sort of "good humoured" indifference. This, in spite of the missionary's deliberate adoption of the native costume. It is to be noted that the adolescent protagonist Bakha meets Hutchinson immediately before he witnesses the people's response to Gandhi. Colonel Hutchinson, the Christian evangelist, attempt to catch young Bakha and convert him to Christianity. Bakha does not understand the Colonel's preachings but he follows him to the Church in the hope of getting a pair of trousers—the symbol of English life. But Bakha slips off from Colonel's sight as he listens to his wife's contemptuous remarks on Bhangis and Chamars. Even an illiterate boy like Bakha can clearly see the contradictions between what Hutchinson sermonizes and what he actually lives. Colonel Hutchinson is not successful in winning the natives to his ways.

But the point at which the implications of decolonization are acutely dramatized is when Bakha is made to listen to the debate on Gandhi's speech[3] concerning untouchability and swaraj (self-governance). According to Gandhi, swaraj is possible only when two of his strongest desires—"emancipation of the untouchables and the protection of the cows"—(127) are fulfilled.

Two antithetical perspectives are presented on Gandhian ideas. The first perspective is that Gandhi is a 'humbug,' and a 'hypocrite' (because "in one breath he says he wants to abolish untouchability and in the other he asserts that he is in orthodox Hindu" 127), anti-democratic in spirit and old-fashioned in his ideas like 'Swadeshi' and 'Spinning Wheel.' This view is contradicted by another: "Gandhi is by far the greatest liberating force of our age" (128). The first view is held by Barrister Bashir, who with his English education, outfit and ideas, precisely answers to Sartre's description of "native elite" manufactured by "European elite."

The one who opposes Mr. Bashir is the poet Iqbal Nath Sarasher significantly dressed in the native manner. With his "delicate feline face, illuminated by sparkling, dark eyes and long, black curly hair... dressed in flowing Indian robes" the poet supports Gandhi's ideas but differs with him in his attitude towards the adoption of technology for the progress of India. Although Gandhi rejects the machine, his follower Iqbal Sarasher asserts: "I shall go against Gandhi there and accept it. And I am sure in time to come all will learn to love it. And we shall beat our enslavers in their own game" (128).

It is important to note that the great debate regarding the prospects of a nation and its people is presented not through an intellectual, but through the consciousness of the *adolescent* Bakha.

In a colonial context, the keepers of native culture, as well as the disseminators of "superior" culture impose great demands on youth. Hence the role of the youth in any struggle against colonial oppression becomes pivotal. In *Weep Not, Child*, Njoroge's brother Boro joins the Mau-Mau.[4] Such young ones, considered the biggest threat to the colonial government, become prime targets of its troops and the home guards. While the missionaries in schools are busy colonizing the young minds with western civilization, the home guards in the forest are busy killing not only those who have turned into Mau-Mau fighters but also those who are suspected to have joined the movement. This is why Njoroge—a suspect—is expelled from school and brutally assaulted by the police. Njoroge's father, who is tortured and castrated by the police for allegedly murdering a native collaborator of the colonial rule, laments: "They don't want an old man's blood ... They—want—the—young—blood" (123). Incidentally, during the Mau-Mau movement, Ngugi was a schoolboy—about Njoroge's (*Weep Not, Child*) age.[5] As a boy he had known school children to assist the "forest fighters" by smuggling arms.

All this must suggest that Anand and Ngugi saw great scope for unfolding momentous social and political events through the personal dramas of their young heroes. In other words, social and political conflicts unravel themselves in the development of boys like Bakha and Waiyaki.

One may briefly examine in this context the manner in which the central conflicts operate in *The River Between*. Chapter one of the novel describes two ridges—Kameno and Makuyu—whose very appearances suggest a rivalry for leadership in the Gikuyu region. But this antagonism of the ridges starts getting dramatized in Chapter Two, in the quarrel between two boys, Kinuthia and Kamau. Kinuthia belongs to one ridge and Kamau to the other. The fight is sparked off because Kamau has jeered at Kinuthia's father who died poor and Kinuthia has called the other's father "a convert to the white man." Kamau calls Kinuthia a "beggar" and is in the bargain dubbed "white man's slave" (5). The expression "white man's slave," according to David Cook and Michael Okenimpke, refers to a convert in a country where Christianity has made recent entry (*Explorations*, 26). This seemingly trivial episode actually suggests the impoverishment and slavishness of people under colonial rule, and introduces the central conflict between the two main ridges of the Gikuyu land. The chief representatives of the ridges are Waiyaki—whose follower to the end Kinuthia is, and Kamau, Waiyaki's competitor throughout. Chege, (Waiyaki's father) and Kabonyi (Kamau's father) are of course there as important figures in the clash of values. Later on, Waiyaki's dream of resolving the discord between the two ridges is but consistent with the role that he had played in Chapter Two as arbiter between two wrangling companions Kinuthia and Kamau. The entire book offers extended versions—in terms of social and political significances—of this early episode. Clifford Robson in his book, *Ngugi Wa Thiong'o* makes a somewhat similar remark:

"What on the surface appears to be a quarrel between children contains in embryo the shape of future conflict" (6).

The present discussion, it is hoped, turns to better account Robson's insightful but passing remark, by making a subtle shift in emphasis: Ngugi specially chooses the very young to introduce and develop the collision of cultures in Gikuyu land. This clash of cultures is heightened over customs relating to attainment of puberty and adulthood—circumcision and baptism. For the Makuyu group—whose important figure is Joshua, devoted to the new faith as only a convert can be—the most important issue centering on the young in baptism; for the Kameno group, the corresponding mandatory subject is circumcision. One needs to note well that the most passionate concern of these ridges are those relating to circumcision and baptism. The ridges representing the old and the new faiths are paradoxically separated by the river Honia (meaning 'cure'). The bank of the river serves as a common site for the ritual ceremonies of baptism and circumcision, which are conducted around the same time—Christmas—particularly on Sundays. Educated in the Siriana Mission School, Waiyaki has his hesitations regarding the old custom of circumcision. But young Muthoni's rebellion against her staunch Christian father Joshua, assist Waiyaki's acceptance of the circumcision rite. In a most decided way, Muthoni leaves her father and crosses over to the other ridge to her aunt and undergoes circumcision. The father disowns his daughter immediately (and totally). An unruffled Muthoni dies a few days after her circumcision. But her poise lends unquestionable strength to her character. Facing death, she asserts in the most collected manner that she has seen Christ ("Tell Nyambura I see Jesus," 75). The conviction of young Muthoni's personal vision easily surpasses the dogmatic Joshua's vociferous proselytization. Trained in a Christian school but deeply influenced by the pagan ritual undergone by the native Christian's daughter, Waiyaki struggles for the rest of the novel to achieve the blend of the old and the new faiths—an almost impossible, nevertheless noble ideal. As already noted, the grasp of these cultural conflicts and dilemmas is from the vantage point of adolescence.

The novels of Anand and Ngugi are affirmations of an awakening. The need for rejuvenation of the culture under colonial rule, the need for a national awakening, is effectively expressed through the awakening consciousness of the "adolescent" mind. That is why Anand describes Bakha as a "child of Modern India" (*Untouchable,* 10).

Adolescence, a vital stage in the development of an individual, denotes a period of transition from childhood to adulthood. It indicates a significant change in the individual's physical nature as well as in his mental, emotional and social attitudes. At the threshold of adulthood, the adolescent arrives at a heterosexual attitude—which is what the attainment of physical and social puberty mainly implies. The search for identity becomes crucial at this point of one's life. Erik Erikson in *Childhood and Society* captures the 'adolescent' predicament:

> The adolescent mind is essentially a mind of the *moratorium,* a psychosocial stage between childhood and adulthood, and between the morality learned by a child, and ethics to be developed by the adult. It is an ideological mind—and, indeed it is the ideological outlook of the society that speaks most clearly to the adolescent who is eager to be affirmed by his peers and is ready to be confirmed by rituals, creeds and programs, which at the same time define what is evil, uncanny and inimical (263).

Any child's eagerness for adulthood is understandable. Erikson's observation makes clear to us why initiation rites are central to an individual as well as to a community. Waiyaki (in *The River Between*) does not like to be thought young for he considers himself capable of making "decisions like a man" (47). His desire to play the game "Demi Ma Mathathi" is but an expression of his eagerness to "become a man" (47). Similarly, Njoroge in *Weep Not, Child,* "always longed for the day he would be a man" (47). He perceives manhood as a way of finding "freedom." This is seen in his desire to "touch circumcised girls;" for, as a boy he is prohibited to mix with them. Bakha in *Untouchable* and Munoo in *Coolie,* share with Waiyaki and Njoroge the longing to become *men*. Adulthood signifies for them 'dignity' and 'freedom'. As a child, Bakha's desire was to become a 'washerman' (75) or a Sahib, on growing up. Munoo in *Coolie* "would have liked to shave his beard with a sharp, long razor of his master's" but "there was yet no hair on his cheeks or his chin. He wished he would grow up soon and have a beard. He wanted to become a man" (91). When Munoo is refused a coolie's job in the grain market because his frame is considered too young to carry the sacks of grain, he feels humiliated and is indignant about himself. He muses: "when will I grow up and be a strong man?" (124). Becoming a *man* is necessary for his survival in the competitive world of coolies. Lalu's ambition (in *The Village*) is to "grow up quickly and be a man," to "learn to plough like his (elder) brothers" (87).

Anand's and Ngugi's adolescents are no different from adolescents in general. But they are adolescents placed at 'special' moments in the histories of their countries; their yearning for adulthood is dramatized in a socio-cultural arena of heightened historical significance. One may recall what Anand says in *Apology for Heroism*: "The era to which I was born was... the historical turning point of my country" (71).

It would be rewarding to consider briefly, from this perspective, the use of myths by Ngugi and Anand. In a discussion of *The River Between* T.N. Dhar observes:

> The single most interesting thing about the coming of the whites in Ngugi's fiction is that he mythologies the event (69).

The Gikuyu seer Mugo had prophesied, in the remote past, the coming of the whites: "There shall come a people with clothes like butterflies," "disrupting the peace and the ordered life of the country" (*The River Between*, 19). "Mugo often said you could not cut the butterflies with a Panga. You could not spear them until you learnt and knew their ways and movement" (20).

Dhar's observation becomes meaningful in the light of the argument of this thesis. Standing at the threshold of adulthood, and at a special period in the history of the country, native adolescents like Waiyaki and Bakha face two sets of traditions/values, most often presented in the form of myths. Mythification and demythification are invariably at work at the setting-in and exit of the colonizer. The colonizers as well as the natives involve themselves in mythifying and demythifying each other. But these sets of conflicting myths address themselves most compellingly to the adolescent mind. Which are the myths that are desirable, and which are those that are to be eschewed? Adolescents like Waiyaki and Njoroge face this choice crucially at puberty. Therefore, the centrality of circumcision in Ngugi's fiction. In the acquisition of one set of myths and the discarding of certain others, is interwoven the freedom and future of the native culture. Such a need may actuate an amalgamation of different sets of myths and values. On the day of Waiyaki's 'second birth'[6] ceremony, Chege is eager to bequeath a sense of heritage to his son, by relating him to the seer Mugo and to his promise. The seer had uttered: "Salvation shall come from the hills. From the blood that flows in me, I say from the same tree a son shall rise. And his duty shall be to lead and save the people!" (*The River Between*, 20). If Waiyaki must acquire the white man's learning, it is in order to realize Mugo's prediction. 'Arise', the father exhorts Waiyaki, "Heed the prophecy. Go to the Mission place. Learn all the wisdom and all the secrets of the white man. But do not follow his vices. Be true to your people and the ancient rites" (20).

Similarly, Njoroge's (in *Weep Not, Child*) faith in future shows itself in the way he attempts a reconstruction of myths:

> It did not make much difference that he had come to identify Gikuyu with Adam and Mumbi with Eve. To this God, all men and women were united by one strong bond of brotherhood. And with all this, there was growing up in his heart a feeling that Gikuyu people whose land had been taken by white men, were no other than the children of Israel about whom he read in the Bible. So although all men were brothers, the black people had a special Mission to the world because they

> were the chosen people of God. This explained his brother's remark that Jomo was the black Moses (49).

Njoroge's development is based both on traditional folklore and the Bible, specially on the Old Testament characters like David, Job and Moses. He looks up to Jomo Kenyatta as the saviour of black people and listens with great interest to the stories about Jomo:

> Njoroge listened keenly as they talked of Jomo. Already he felt intimate with this man. For Njoroge was sure that he had read about him in the Old Testament. Moses had led the children of Israel from Misri to the Promised Land. And because black people were really the children of Israel, Moses was no other than Jomo himself. It was obvious (50).

In *Untouchable*, where decolonization is in an advanced stage (in contrast to the situation in *The River Between* where it has just begun) there are two sets of myths and legends that present themselves before Bakha. The "Sola topi" in the barracks had been a symbol of status for Bakha. There are various stories and beliefs regarding the topi: it is a symbol of the sahib's authority over the regiment; it is thought to be imprisoned, since its owner, a white man, could not be imprisoned for a murder he committed; "it belonged to an officer who had just gone into the grounds" (85) and would be returning to take it. The younger children believe this last version and are scared because of the association made between ghosts and white sahibs. However, the topi has generally been understood as a symbol of status. Bakha too as a child is fascinated by the topi. But as he grows, his attitude changes slightly. Significantly, on the verge of adulthood, he is attracted to it as a "lover":

> Bakha had for years looked with longing at the sola topi... Ever since he was a little boy he had contemplated it with the wonder-struck gaze of the lover and the devotee. Whenever he was given the chance of going out sweeping in the compounds... he could steal glances at the object he coveted... (*Untouchable*, 86).

The topi is still an object of status for Bakha, but disassociated from any idea of the supernatural. The other set of myths that presents itself to Bakha can be best illustrated through one example: the rendering of Gandhi's personality. Gandhi

> is an 'avatar' of the Gods Vishnu and Krishna. Only recently he (Bakha) had heard that a spider had woven a web in the house of the Lat Sahib (Lord Sahib) at Dilli (Delhi), making a portrait of the sage, and writing his name under it in English. That was said to be a warning to the Sahibs to depart from Hindustan, since God almighty himself had sent a message through a little insect that Gandhi was to be the Maharaja of the whole Hindustan. That the spider's web appeared in the Lat Sahib's Kothi was surely significant. And, they said, no sword could cut his body, no bullet could pierce his skin, no fire could scorch him! (117).

Bakha does not at all question this description of Gandhi. The confidence with which a nation awaits its independence from foreign rule gets expressed through the unhesitant and total acceptance of God's signature through a spider.

A most interesting aspect of the fictional works of Anand and Ngugi is that the need for liberation from an oppressed foreign rule gets artistically woven into the young adolescents' zeal for adult, independent status. The desire and need for adulthood involves naturally the need for independent identity and dignity. In other words, the adulthood-aspirations of boys like Waiyaki, Njoroge, Bakha, Munoo and Lalu are seen as mirroring their societies' struggle for liberation from oppressive foreign rule to attain 'nationhood'—independence. During the passage from adolescence to adulthood an initiate is separated from childhood, but not fully integrated into adulthood; the bewilderment and confusion that he experiences during the transition are reflected in the political turbulence of that society. Fredric Jameson in "Third-World Literature in the Era of Multinational Capitalism" aptly sums up the situation thus:

> Third-World texts... necessarily project a political dimension in the form of national allegory: the story of

> private individual destiny is always an allegory of the embattled situation of the public in Third-World culture and society (68).

It is fascinating to see how this truth is realized in fictional terms by Ngugi and Anand.

Ngugi's grasp of the transitional nature of the Gikuyu society expresses itself fictionally through the transitional stage in the life of an adolescent like Waiyaki. The incorporation of the individual into community life is an important act in Gikuyu society, and hence the centrality of the circumcision rites in Gikuyu life. In fact, circumcision is the biggest of events, before which one has to undergo the 'second birth' ceremony. While the second birth ceremony leads the individual only 'to the threshold of maturity and understanding' (tentative initiation—as Mordecai Marcus would say—) the circumcision takes the individual firmly into maturity and understanding (decisive initiation).[7] After the circumcision ceremony (that involves the process of separation, transition and incorporation)[8] the novice becomes a full member of the society. Note the description of Waiyaki's circumcision:

> All his life Waiyaki had waited for this day, for this very opportunity to reveal his courage like a man... The knife produced a thin sharp pain as it cut through the flesh. The surgeon had done his work. Blood trickled freely on to the ground, sinking into the soil. Henceforth a religious bond linked Waiyaki to the earth, as if his blood was an offering (*The River Between*, 45).

Waiyaki thus symbolically belongs to the land and to the tribe as a whole. According to the elders who watch the spectacle, Waiyaki's ability to endure the pain is confirmation of his resistance to the corrupting influence of the white man's ways. The circumcision rites in *The River Between* most emphatically relate the adolescent to his land. With the perception that he is related through blood to the earth, Waiyaki's adolescent consciousness enlarges to an adult consciousness.

A more telling example (of this kind of growth) is presented in *Matigari*. Standing on the bank of the river, Matigari the eponymous hero of the novel remembers the ceremonial occasion on which he, along with others underwent circumcision:

> The water had numbed their skin, so that none of them felt the pain as the knife cut into the flesh. Before this moment they were mere boys, but by the time they unclenched their fists, they were men. Their blood mingled with the soil, and they became patriots, ready for the armed struggle to come (4).

The affirmation or denial of adulthood to a people is a reliable pointer to the feeling for nationality and self-governance; self-governance must presume recognition of national territory as homeland. Ngugi's tale "The Martyr" (*Secret Lives and Other Stories*) set during the Mau-Mau movement should serve to illustrate this. The story opens with the news that two English settlers—Mr. and Mrs. Garstones—have been murdered by native 'gangsters,' with the help of Garstones' servant. This deed is symptomatic of the general 'violence' that makes every white settler in the land insecure. Mrs. Hill, in whose house the murder is discussed, is a 'liberal' who keeps reiterating that "the natives are obedient at heart and all you needed was to treat them kindly" (0). She herself treats her servant 'kindly,' but she does not know that her liberal, kind ways have taken her servant Njoroge to the limits of his hatred for settlers, and especially for Mrs. Hill, and he has secretly contacted the 'gangsters' (the Mau-Mau fighters referred to as 'Ihii' or 'Freedom Boys' by the natives). The plan is to kill Mrs. Hill at night and Njoroge has agreed to lead them up to her door. Mrs. Hill is ignorant of this development but despite her articulation of kind treatment to natives, her mind is impressed by one detail: it was Garstones' servant that had rendered the master and mistress vulnerable. Njoroge has served her for more than a decade—but could there not be a repeat performance of disloyalty in her own house? So she arms herself that night with a pistol. Meanwhile Njoroge, 'betrays' not his employer, but the 'Freedom Boys,' for he cannot imagine killing Mrs. Hill who is a mother of two children. He gives the 'Freedom Boys' the slip and goes up to Mrs. Hill's door and knocks. His intention is to warn Mrs. Hill against the 'Freedom Boys.' Night has advanced and Mrs. Hill's mind is full of only the circumstances of Garstones' death. Sweating with fear, she shoots and kills her servant. "She did not know she had in fact killed her saviour" (47). The morning's papers are full of praise for the white woman who has single handedly a "gang of fifty" and has even killed one!

It is interesting that the people of the land are treated as *boys*. The servants are *invariably* referred to as "houseboys" by the whites. Njoroge has been with Mrs. Hill for ten years and he is still a 'houseboy!' In fact this 'houseboy' is a middle-aged man with "two wives and a number of children" (44). Any reflection on the houseboy as a 'man' appears ridiculous to Mrs. Hill:

> She thought of Njoroge. A queer boy. Had he many wives? Had he a large family? It was surprising to find that she had lived with him so long, yet had never thought of these things... Even now it seemed ridiculous to think of her houseboy as a father with a family (47).

In a subtle manner, the freedom fighters who oppose the settlers as well as the servants—in short, all natives—are retained in boyhood. Otherwise started, the white settlers incline to deny adult status to all natives, be they servants or 'resenters.' They are all either 'Freedom Boys' or 'houseboys' or 'Shamba boys.' A sensitive reader knows that the practice of referring to male natives (irrespective of their age) as 'boys' is but a dehumanizing device of the colonizing instinct. Awareness of territory as homeland is enacted through the genuine 'adult' sensibilities of the characters. The liberality of Mrs. Hill is mentioned alongside her ownership of vast plantations, while the brickhouse she has constructed out of kindness for her 'houseboy' allows just enough room for Njoroge to go to bed without stretching his arms:

> Yet it has here, *here*, that he with two wives and a number of children had to live, had in fact lived for more than five years. So crammed! Yet Mrs. Hill thought that she had done enough by just having the houses built with brick (44).

And behind the change of Njoroge's heart regarding killing Mrs. Hill is *his* acknowledgement of Mrs. Hill's status of adulthood (whether she deserves it or not):

> He knew she had loved her husband.... Then the children! He had known them. He had seen them grow up like any other children. *Almost like his own.* They loved their parents, and Mrs. Hill had always been so tender with them, so loving. He thought of them in England, wherever that was, *fatherless* and *motherless*...
>
> And then he realized, too suddenly, that he could not do it... Mrs. Hill had suddenly crystallized into a woman, *a wife... and above all a mother*... He could not kill a mother (45).

In the tale, the native Njoroge dies and the settler Mrs. Hill survives. But a sensitive reader understands that Ngugi, without approving violence, is questioning the moral right of the white to stay on the African land. The moral claims to the land are examined in terms of the readiness to admit adult/human status to the other.

Similarly, the nation's aspirations and struggle for independence in *Untouchable* are comprehended through Bakha's advance towards adulthood. Since untouchables are kept outside the pale of society, there is no 'community' into which Bakha can grow up; adult status is denied to untouchables, as it is for slaves. There can be no social or psychological dimensions to the 'puberty' of young untouchables like Bakha and his sister Sohini. The poignancy of the denial adulthood is achieved through frustrating the scopes for achieving even physical mystery. It is true that at the age of eighteen Bakha has developed the conspicuous physical features of an adult. In spite of "the poor nourishment he got, he had developed into a big, strong man, broad-shouldered, heavy-hipped, supple-bodied" (14). But his physical growth or physical maturity is one that is not meaningfully realized; rather it seems aimlessly attained. Bakha's strong body may enable him to perform better the serf's work, but it cannot earn him full membership of society. In spite of the generous description of Bakha's physical frame, there is hardly any hint in the novel regarding his marital opportunities. Bakha's youth and physical development is built up solely to be frustrated. This is best delineated in the episode concerning the marriage of Ram Charan's sister. Bakha had, in his childhood, played husband to this girl. That was in a game that Bakha and the other children had played when Bakha was just eight and the girl about four. The role assigned to him is one that Bakha has cherished all along. He has since then watched Ram Charan's sister grow up into a "tall girl with a face as brown as ripe wheat and hair as black as rain clouds." We are told that he "always felt proud of having once acted as her husband" (74). However, the role of husband to a woman who can be a match, (in sheer physical energy at least) is one that will never materialize in his real life. It is on the day of her wedding... a time when he himself is at the threshold of adulthood—that Bakha fully becomes aware of his lowly position in society. Bakha's unexpressed ambition for adult status is violently punctured as Ram Charan in his boyish manner knocks "the bottom out of that ambition by telling Bakha though he (Ram Charan) touched him and played with him, he was a Hindu, while Bakha was a mere sweeper." Bakha was too young at that time "to understand the distinction implied in the washer boy's arrogant claim" but on the day when Ram Charan's sister is married, Bakha perceives adult/social status as an impossibility: "now he knew that there were degrees of castes among the low-caste, and that he was the lowest" (76). The way the episode ends is significant:

> He (Bakha) was feeling quite *detached from the human world*, bathed in a sort of unadulterated melancholy (78). (Emphasis added)

Ram Charan is from a low-caste, only one rank above Bakha's and yet his attitude to Bakha is marked by arrogance. How much more insensitive and hostile then, would be the attitude of the social system to Bakha's aspirations for adulthood? A small episode in the novel should serve as an apt illustration. Bakha is on the streets, shouting his lowly status as untouchable, in order to 'warn' people to avoid his contact.

For a moment he is distracted by a Sikh craftsman fixing cheap German lithographs of Hindu deities into "expensive-looking frames" (48).

> The picture of an English-woman, *very scantily dressed, and reclining with a flower in her hand, seduced* Bakha's eyes away from the Hindu deities. The shopkeeper, *noticing the basket and broom* in his hand, gave him a *stern look of disapproval* and asked him to move on. The sweeper-boy lifted his face and pushing ahead called; posh, posh, sweeper coming... (48). (Emphasis added)

Around this event, there is an abundance of detail to which Bakha's adolescent consciousness is painfully sensitive. The passage is studded with details related to women: cheap jewellery, ear-rings, nose-rings, hair-flowers; and there is a seller of "cloth-remnants" and bangle-sellers shaking their glass-wares "to dazzle and attract young brides." Also the women themselves are seen talking from their "heaving, big bosoms." What is to be noted is that Bakha must, through shouting his lowly place, warn these women thronging the street not to be touched by him, and the shopkeepers too must "appraise the women of the coming of the untouchable" (48).

Such a thwarted adulthood may partly explain Bakha's attitude to his sister Sohini. We are informed that his feelings for Sohini were "not altogether that of a brother for a sister" (20) and he loathes the imaginary sight of Sohini walking along with her would-be-husband. There "seemed no difference to his naked mind between his own feeling for her and what might be a husband's love" (55). Such confused feelings are not unexpected in a society that denies human status to individuals. The obstructions in the way of Bakha's adulthood are in fact obstructions to his human status.

The 'right to freedom' of a society is expressed through the right to human status of its individuals—which means granting full membership to them. But a person like Bakha (who is kept outside the pale of society) can be initiated only through indoctrination—since the social atmosphere denies experience to him. Hence the significance of Gandhi and his speech in the novel.

Gandhi arrives at that moment when Bakha's feeling of frustration is most biting. The Mahatma raises his right hand and blesses the crowd with "gentle benediction." The effect is intense. It is "as if he had sent an electric shock through the mass of humanity gathered at his feet" (121).

Bakha for once forgets that he is an untouchable. "In the stillness of moment, Bakha forgot all the details of his experience during the day, the touched man, the priest... his father, Chota, Ram Charan... the missionary and his wife" (122). Gandhi's speech is about untouchability, which for a seer like him is about individuals' freedom as well as the nation's:

> As you all know, while we are asking for freedom from the grip of a foreign nation, we have ourselves, for centuries, trampled underfoot millions of human beings without feeling the slightest remorse of our inequity (123).

It is not a coincidence that Gandhi speaks on the very subject—emancipation of untouchables—that centrally involves Bakha.[9] To Bakha who has felt totally separated from the human world, Gandhi appears a unifying force, a link between him and the rest of humanity. Standing in the crowd that is magnetically drawn to Gandhi, he thinks he is "in the midst of humanity, which included him in its fold and yet debarred him from entering into... a contact with it. Gandhi alone united him with them." The entire thrust of Gandhi's speech is in the direction of leading untouchables ("low dregs of humanity") towards human dignity. Bakha becomes more attentive when Gandhi says that "Untouchability is the greatest blot of Hinduism" (116). The story of the untouchable boy Uka related by Gandhi engaged Bakha's entire being for two reasons: (1) Bakha feels it is his story, in which Gandhi grants human status to a sweeper (2). Uka's story in a way speaks of Gandhi's own growth to maturity. Throughout his boyhood Gandhi had questioned why physical contact with untouchables was forbidden. Gandhi has grown to adulthood "smilingly protesting" that untouchability had no religious sanction; he had regularly touched untouchables on his way to school. Bakha's interest in Gandhi's own story waxes. Gandhi speaks of the need to consider human beings as equals in order to qualify for spiritual freedom. It is this need that is expressed in his rejection, in case he is born again, of any other status in society but the untouchable's. Bakha gets even more involved in Gandhi's address when Gandhi says there is an eighteen-year-old Brahmin boy (and Bakha too is eighteen) in his ashram who does a sweeper's work. "Bakha felt thrilled. A tremor went down his spine" (125). "Swaraj" or freedom from foreign rule has no meaning for Gandhi as long as untouchables are treated as slaves by Hindus. Hence his appeal to grant them human status.

Gandhi's voice is like a whisper, yet it ensures clarity to the words he utters and has the effect of religious indoctrination (in a positive sense) for an initiate. In the awakening of the lowliest in society like Uka and Bakha is the possibility of the nation's awakening.

The moment of the sage's prayer is Bakha's moment of waking up to the human realm, as it were. Bakha hears "each syllable of the Hindu hymn" (122) that is sung at Gandhi's prayer.

The hymn most appropriately is an appeal to the human soul to awaken:

> The dawn is here, O traveller, arise;
> Past is the night, ...
> Lost is the soul that sleeps
> The sleepless one finds peace beyond all woe
> Oh, waken!... (122).

A self-evident, perhaps therefore unnoticed aspect of Anand's and Ngugi's works concerns the starting point of their narratives. Quite a few of their tales begin to unfold around dawn. "Dawn diffused through cracks in the wall into the hut" (1). That is how the yarn of *A Grain of Wheat* starts unrolling. *Petals of Blood,* which has four protagonists with their own tales, offers four inaugurations of the narrative. Each strand of this fabric starts around dawn:

> They came for him (Munira) on Sunday. *He had just returned from a night's vigil* on the mountains. He was resting in his bed... when two police constables... knocked at the door (2).
>
> Abdulla sat on a chair... He felt strangely calm *after a night's vigil* (3).
>
> Karega was fast asleep. *He had come from an all-night executive meeting* of Ilmorog Theng'eta Breweries Union. He heard a knock at the door. He leapt out his bed in his pyjamas (3). (Emphasis added)
>
> One newspaper, the *Daily Mouthpiece* brought out a special issue with a banner headline: MZIGO, CHUI, KIMERA MURDERED (4).

It may be safely assumed that the *Daily Mouthpiece* is a morninger. The action proper of *Devil on the Cross* begins thus: "On Friday morning Waringa was dismissed from the job... On Saturday morning (she)... was visited by the landlord" (10). Thrown out by her landlord, she starts her journey to her parents' house in Ilmorog the same morning. In the opening scene of *Matigari* the sun is "just rising" (3) when the hero is returning home from the mugumo tree. We are not explicitly told that it is morning when the action commences in *The River Between*, but the impression, if one goes by the magnitude of the sunlight, is that the sun is ascending, not descending: "If you strained your eyes and pierced into the misty distance you could see the land of Ukabi" (4).

These beginnings interestingly parallel those of Anand's tales. At the commencement of *Untouchable* Bakha lies "half-awake in the morning of an autumn day" (9) and he wakes up as the "sharp wind" blowing from the brook at dawn" penetrates "his skin" (10). In the opening scene of *Coolie*, Munoo who is about to leave his village, has taken out cattle under a "morning sun" (1). Computing the time Gangu takes to reach the plantation after alighting the train, we must infer that the novel begins at morning. The opening scene of *The*

Village has the morning-setting. Alighting from the train at Nandpur station, old Nihal Singh walks towards his village. A little later, we read that the old man "lifted his eyes, undimmed by age, to the sum which had already risen high in the eastern sky" (11). The first pages of *The Sword and the Sickle* show Lalu waking up from sleep in the Bombay-Peshawar Mail to these words, "Awake... Awake..." "What time is it?" asks Lalu of a companion. "Dawn time" is the reply, "must be around five O' clock" (1).

It is not the mere fact of dawn figuring in the beginning of so many tales that calls for notice but that its frequency of such beginnings is sufficient to assume significance. Such a beginning as has just been discussed is quite in tune with the strategies Anand and Ngugi employ to relate personal awakening to adulthood with national awakening. The awakening is to harsh realities. None of the works by the two writers ends in easy and false happiness. This may explain partly, why many of their novels close with the approach of night. *Untouchable* ends this way: "The sun descended, the pale, the purple, the mauve of the horizon blended into darkest sky" (132). *Coolie* ends with Munoo's death "in the early hours of one unreal, white night" (282). *Two Leaves and a Bud* closes with Gangu's death in "scarlet darkness" (273). The final scene of *The Village* shows Lalu getting ready to go across the black waters: "He... looked across the sea-waves to the horizon where the sun haze descended in a mist"[10] (247). *Across the Black Waters* draws to a close as Lalu is taken captive by the Germans after the final battle fought in the night. The pattern is similar in Ngugi's works. The *Devil on the Cross* ends in the latter half of the day with Waringa killing her seducer and walking out of his house in a heroic manner. The *River Between* and *Weep Not, Child* end with the night encroaching on the land.

'Dawn' and 'dusk' are periods of transition, and hence quite appropriate to begin and end the accounts of transition on the individual and national scales.

NOTES

1. Ngugi recalls in *Homecoming* how the boys in the Mission School, where he was a student himself, were trained to be "good responsible leaders" of the people, and how they were "being groomed to become a buffer state between the propertied white rulers and the harsh realities under which the African peasants and workers lived" (49).
2. See Jomo Kenyatta's *Facing Mount Kenya.* (136-7).
3. Carefully drawn from the speech Gandhi delivered at the Suppressed Classes Conference in Ahmedabad on 13 April, 1921. Saros Cowasjee (in the essay, "Mulk Raj Anand: The Fusion of History and Fiction") notes its significance in the text by differentiating between the actual speech and the fictionalized version. He finds the actual speech disappointing but its fictional rendition captivating to the reader.
4. Also called Kenya Land and Freedom Army (KLFA). The origin of the name 'Mau-Mau' remains obscure. David Maughan—Brown, in his detailed study of the fictional and non-fictional works dealing with Mau-Mau informs that the expression 'Mau-Mau' has no literal meaning in either Gikuyu or Swahili language. According to him the origin of the term is attributed not to the members of the movement but to the colonizer. Brown's own version is that Mau-Mau was 'an armed struggle waged by the Gikuyu peasantry against the British Colonial forces from 1952-57.' Defeated militarily, the movement nevertheless hastened the independence of Kenya, opines the author. There is an interesting explanation of the coinage, Mau-Mau, which some of my Kenyan students revealed to me. According to their elucidation it stands for

   M — Muzungu — European/Whiteman
   a — Aende — To go
   u — Ulaya — England

   M — Mwafia — An Africa
   a — Apate — To get
   u — Uhuru — Freedom

   Mau-Mau remains a much-debated issue in Kenyan literary and political history. Ngugi's response to it is marked by ambiguities. He gives a balanced view of Mau-Mau in his fictional works set in the Colonial period (*The River Between, Weep Not, Child* and *A Grain of Wheat*), but one notices a slight shift in his attitude to Mau-Mau in novels like *Petals of Blood, Devil on the Cross* and *Matigari*, which deal with neocolonial situations in Kenya. In these works Mau-Mau is spoken of as a "Heroic struggle of the people," "Spirit of Kenya's peasants and workers." In works like *Writers in Politics, Barrel of a Pen: Resistance to Repression in Neocolonial Kenya* and *Moving the Centre*, it is seen as the "starting point" of the coming struggle against all oppressive forces.

5. David Cook and Michael Okenimpke (in *Ngugi Wa Thiong'o: An Exploration of His Writings*) see Njoroge as a fictional enactment of Ngugi's childhood and adolescent life: Ngugi's father was an 'ahoi' (squatter); so is Njoroge's father. One of Ngugi's brothers joined Mau-Mau; Njoroge's brother Boro does the same. Another brother of Ngugi was in detention—which is the fate of Njoroge's brother Kori. Siriana Mission in which Njoroge was a pupil is the fictional equivalent of Ngugi's Alliance High School meant to manufacture the native elite.
6. This rite is performed by cutting a thin cord taken from a slaughtered goat and tied to the human child's mother. The act symbolizes the severing of the umbilical cord and the child's separation from his mother and his incorporation into new world. The child's head is then shorn off hair. After a ceremonial dip in the river, he comes out 'clean'. The second birth ceremony makes the child eligible for 'circumcision.'
7. See Mordecai Marcus's "What is an Initiation Story?".
8. See Van Gennep's *Rites of Passage* (11).
9. Bakha is modelled on an untouchable boy whom Anand knew in his childhood. Anand describes the boy thus: "a rare human being whom I had known from my childhood and adored as a hero because he was physically like a God." See his essay "The Story of My Experiment with a White Lie."
10. The sight of the "morning sun" on the last page of the novel is Lalu's imaginative picture of his village scene. This should not be mistaken for the end of the narrative's action.

WORKS CITED

Achebe, Chinua, *Things Fall Apart.* London: Heinemann, 1958.

Anand, Mulk Raj. *Across the Black Waters.* 1940. Bombay: Popular-Kutub, 1955.

Anand, Mulk Raj. *Apology for Heroism.* 1946. Bombay: Popular-Kutub, 1980.

Anand, Mulk Raj. *Coolie.* 1936. New Delhi: Penguin, 1993.

Anand, Mulk Raj. *Morning Face.* Bombay: Popular-Kutub, 1968.

Anand, Mulk Raj. "The Story of My Experiment with a White Lie". Indian Literature. 10.3 (1967) Rpt. in *Critical Essays on Indian Writing in English.* Ed. M.K. Naik, *et al.* Dharwar: Karnataka U, 1968.

Anand, Mulk Raj. *The Sword and the Sickle.* 1942. New Delhi: Arnold-Heinemann, 1984.

Anand, Mulk Raj. *The Village.* London: Jonathan Cape. 1939.

Anand, Mulk Raj. *Two Leaves and a Bud.* 1937. New Delhi: Arnold Associates, 1994.

Anand, Mulk Raj. *Untouchable.* 1935. Mysore: Geetha Book House, 1995.

Cook, David, and Michael Okenimpke. *Ngugi Wa Thiong'o: An Exploration of His Writings.* London: Heinemann, 1983.

Cowasjee, Saros. "Mulk Raj Anand: The fusion of History and Fiction." *Subjects Worthy Fame.* ed. A.L. MacLeod. New Delhi: Sterling, 1989.

Dhar, T.N. "The Complex Web of the Colonial Encounter in Ngugi's Fiction." *Colonial Consciousness in Black American, African And Indian Fiction in English.* Ed. Ramesh K. Srivastava, Jalandhar, India: ABS Publications, 1991.

Erikson, Erik H. *Childhood and Society.* 1950. 2nd ed. New York: Norton, 1963.

Fanon, Frantz. *The Wretched of the Earth.* 1961. Trans. Constance Farrington, London: Penguin, 1990.

Jameson, Fredric. "Third-World Literature in the Era of Multinational Capitalism." *Social Text.* Vol. 15 (Fall 1986).

Kenyatta, Jomo. *Facing Mount Kenya.* 1938. Nairobi: East African Educational Publications, 1992.

Maughan-Brown, David. *Land, Freedom and Fiction.* London: Zed Books, 1985.

Marcus, Mordecai. "What is an Initiation Story?" *Journal of Aesthetics and Art Criticism.* 19.2, Winter 1960. *Critical Approaches to Fiction.* Eds. Shiv K. Kumar and Mordecai Marcus.

Palmer, Eustace. *An Introduction to the African Novel.* London: Heinemann, 1972.

Robson, Clifford B. *Ngugi Wa Thiong'o.* London: Macmillan, 1979.

Thiong'o, Ngugi Wa. *A Grain of Wheat.* 1967. London: Heinemann, 1974.

Thiong'o, Ngugi Wa. *Devil on the Cross* (First published in Gikuyu, 1980). London: Heinemann, 1982.

Thiong'o, Ngugi Wa. *Homecoming: Essays on African and Caribbean Literature, Culture and Politics* 1972. London: Heinemann, 1981.

Thiong'o, Ngugi Wa. *Matigari* (First published in Gikuyu, 1987). Nairobi: East African Educational Publishers, rpt. 1994.

Thiong'o, Ngugi Wa. *Petals of Blood.* 1977. London: Heinemann, 1978.

Thiong'o, Ngugi Wa. "The Martyr." *Secret Lives and Other Stories.* Nairobi: East African Educational Publications, 1993.

Thiong'o, Ngugi Wa. *The River Between,* 1965. London: Heinemann, 1981.

Thiong'o, Ngugi Wa. *Weep Not, Child.* 1964. London: Heinemann, 1985.

Van Gennep, Arnold. *Rites of Passage.* 1906. Trans. Monika B. Vizedom and Gabrielle L. Caffe, London: Routledge, 1960.

The Excremental and The Genital

3

Chapter two sought to understand national awakening in terms of the growth of an individual from boyhood to adulthood. It was seen that in the fictional worlds of Mulk Raj Anand and Ngugi, the tensions and bewilderment of youth at the threshold of maturity provide a dependable index to the national situation. The attempt in this chapter is to examine the type of consciousness these writers attribute to their protagonists. The operative consciousness in their worlds is not 'cerebral' but is centered around the loins. This consciousness could be termed 'anal' or 'excremental' in the case of Anand, and 'genital' in Ngugi's case. 'Excremental' and 'genital' are not loaded with the meanings one may associate them with in psychoanalysis. This thesis finds the terms 'excremental' and 'genital' convenient to understand the nature of a special kind of consciousness in the fictional worlds of Anand and Ngugi. Essentially evaluative in nature, this consciousness manifests itself in the interaction of the young heroes with their social and political environments.

It is perhaps better to begin with illustrations and *Coolie* serves the purpose well. The action of the novel starts with the shifting of the fourteen year old protagonist Munoo from Bilaspur village to the city of Sham Nagar and the implications of the drastic change in environment are powerfully worked out in an episode related to excretal activity. In the altered atmosphere, Munoo wakes up to a crisis: he cannot locate any place in and around his master's house to relieve himself. In the village, the first thing the boy did when he woke up in the morning (like all other villagers), was to relieve himself in the open fields. The restrictive nature of the new situation presents itself to him as he hastens, in sheer desperation, to answer nature's call at the wall outside the kitchen door:

> ... the first thing he had always done when he got up every morning in his village home was to run out into the fields and relieve himself, then bathe at the well, come back and eat his food before going to school...
>
> Now he did not know where he should go to relieve himself. There were houses all about, and there were forbidding bungalows cresting the hill. And he could hear people walking on the road.
>
> He did not know where the people in the towns went.
>
> He hastened to the door leading out of the kitchen.
>
> He could not see any latrine attached to the house.
>
> By this time he was in a panic.
>
> He felt he could not control himself any longer.
>
> He felt he was going to spoil his loin cloth.
>
> He ran to the wall outside the house and sat down there (16-17).

He is discovered the act by the mistress of the house. The torrent of abuses, which she rains on him reveals the contempt with which the townspeople regard a rustic:

> 'Vay, you eater of your master! Vay, you shameless brute! You pit! You dog!' the storm burst on his head as ... she appeared at the door, saw him, and unable to bear the sight, withdrew. 'Vay, you shameless, ... vulgar, stupid hillboy! May the vessel of your life never float in the sea of existence! May you die! What have you done! Why didn't you ask me where to go? May you fade away! May you burn! We didn't know we were taking on an animal in our employ, an utter brute, a savage!... Hai! What a horrible, horrible mess he has made outside my door! (17).

Never earlier had Munoo been spotted when easing. He now feels "ashamed to be seen relieving himself in the open" (17). By this time, the whole house is awake. In fact, the inmates of the house are introduced to the readers through their responses to this episode. The master's eldest daughter Sheila, still a young girl, finds the incident funny. The master, Babu Nathoo Ram, angry with Munoo, enquires why his wife did not show the boy where the latrine was. But Bibiji (his wife) is determined that the rustic should not use *their* latrine but the one at the foot of the hill. Dr. Premchand, Babu Nathoo Ram's brother, is sympathetically jocular about the incident. Munoo feels degraded as everybody's attention is drawn to his excretal function.

This, then, is how Munoo, eager to grow to manhood like any other boy of fourteen, wakes up in the city to his real status:

> He realized finally his position in this world. He was to be a slave, a servant who should do the work, all the odd jobs, someone to be abused, even beaten, though as yet it had not come to that. He felt sad; lonely (31).

Alastair Niven in *The Yoke of Pity* has noted the centrality of this section to the novel.

> In most of Anand's novels there comes a crucial moment of realization when the main character fully understands his place in the social order. This moment is the central point of *Untouchable*, but in *Coolie* it comes early on, following on the humiliation he (Munoo) suffers for urinating openly (56).

But it must be stressed that the centrality of this section is due to the image of excretion. One may add that there is no risk of exaggerating the revealing power of this scene. Not only does it illumine the process of self-realization of the main character, but also provides a moral yardstick to measure others in society.

It is through their attitudes to the excretal activity, a bodily function, that people and life-styles are evaluated. Babu Nathoo Ram is an accountant in the Imperial Bank where an Englishman is the reigning officer. Naturally, he and his wife imitate the white man's attitudes and manners. They find fault with Munoo, not on grounds of hygiene, but because they are bothered about their prestige. "We must keep up our prestige" (19) says Bibiji. She fears that the event might damage her reputation to the extent of drawing the white man's attention. After-all her house is in such a location where the white sahibs "pass by" every day. "What will the sahibs think who pass by every morning and afternoon? The Babuji has his prestige to keep up with the sahibs" (17), she complains. Munoo's discovery of the lavatory, a little later, subtly suggests that hygienic considerations in Nathoo Ram's house are not really primary:

> Munoo was scrubbing the utensils with ashes as he sat by the slab, which served both as sink and bathroom, being connected with a drain through a slimy hole in the wall where insects buzzed and the worms crawled. The boy felt the cool odorous draught come in from the drain and dry the sweat on his face. He shifted from where he sat... faced a side door from which the smell of dung assailed his nostrils. 'That must be the lavatory', he thought, 'strange!' (19).

The attitude of Sheila, who is still a girl, is one of amusement. Dr. Premchand is humane, and gently reminds Bibiji that she herself comes from a village.

What one should note in the episode is that assessment of character and society is managed through the 'excretal' images. Munoo's increasing awareness of his lowly status throughout the novel becomes more and more poignant through such images. He helplessly watches his debasement as Bibiji frequently alludes to the incident in the presence of neighbours: "He (Munoo) did not know how to face people if they were all going to be told what he had done this morning" (31).

Munoo's sub-human status is a commentary on not just the social system but the oppressive political situation. Bibiji's view of Munoo is actually derived from the Englishmen's attitude towards the natives, as is revealed in the mock affectation of Dr. Premchand:

> Put it down on this table, black man, you who relieve yourself on the ground! (24).

The colonizer's contempt for the natives finds expression in terms of the latter's excretal habit. Much later in the novel, when Munoo joins as a worker in Sir George White Cotton Mills, he hears the white foreman, Jimmie Thomas, bullying a co-worker and in the process dubbing the whole working class people—who are also totally identified with the natives—as 'black' men 'who relieve themselves on the ground' (174). It is through the image of excrement that Munoo is made to recognize his identity as a servant and this recognition becomes complete in Bombay, when he sees Jimmie Thomas who typifies the attitude of the English towards the natives.

Anand's understanding of the colonial state is seen in the subtle equation he makes between native and labourer, and between white ruler and landlord/capitalist. Munoo cannot but include himself in the class that is abused; his co-workers like Hari and Ratan in 'Sir George White Cotton Mills' are abused by factory foreman Jimmie Thomas, known as 'Chimta Sahib' to the workers. Munoo understands that his own lowly status is but a partial expression of the slave-like status of workers or natives. Hence the significance of Sauda's speech. Sauda, member of the Trade Union Executive Committee apprises the striking workers of the inhuman conditions of the workers for which the capitalists are responsible. "How many of you are not in the grip of the foreman of your factory? Against how many of you have not the hirelings of capitalism wreaked their vengeance?" asks Sauda. Further, he contrasts the rich with the poor:

> The rich and the powerful, the magnificent and the glorious, whose opulence is built on robbery and theft and open warfare, are honoured and admired by the whole world, and by themselves. You, the poor and the humble, you, the meek and the gentle, wretches that you are, swindled out of your rights, and broken in body and soul, you are respected by no one, and you do not respect yourselves (233).

The capitalists here, who move around in Rolls Royces are of course mostly English. The contrast is important, for it shows, Munoo, Ratan and Hari as 'typical' workers and Jimmie

Thomas as a typical capitalist figure. Sauda's speech rouses the indignation of the factory workers by contrasting their actual condition of existence with the white master's contempt for them:

> 'You are the roofless, you are the riceless, spinners of cotton, weavers of thread, sweepers of dust and dirty; you are the workers, the labourers, the millions, of unknown who crawl in and out of factories every day. You are the coolies, *black men who relieve yourselves on the ground*, you are the miserable devils who live twenty a room in broken straw huts and *stinking tenements* (232) (Emphasis added).

Munoo's 'blood boils' with indignation for it is with great passion that Sauda draws pictures of the actualities: fake union leaders (like the Oxford-educated Lalla Onkar Nath) says Sauda, "do not see the wily demon of poverty drag" the labourers "through the murky waters of hell" (232). "Murky waters of hell," is a veiled image of the drainage.

It may be necessary here to point out that Anand's description of rulers does not fall into neat black and white categories. He is ever conscious of the human dignity that any man—black or white—is capable of. That is why we keep seeing in Anand's world honest men like the English Marxist Jackson in *Coolie.* Owen (in *Across the Black Waters*) and Dr. De La Havre in *Two Leaves and a Bud.*

Sauda's description of the state of the workers come only after a vivid dramatization of the actual physical environment of the workers in Bombay. After arriving in Bombay, Munoo is forced to spend the first night on a pavement adjacent to a graveyard. That is the only spot available. He has been guided to that spot by a worker, Hari. Munoo sees the graveyard populated by premature corpses:

> ... he became aware of a hot blast of air which came loaded with the sickly, foetid odour of ghee, sandalwood, urine, sour milk, fish and decaying fruit. He looked in the direction from which the smell oozed. A soft breath, half moan, half sigh, was all he could hear and the

> movement of corpse flinging off its blanket. He looked the other way. There was another coolie turning on his side restlessly and muttering something.
>
> Munoo looked beyond this man, across the road, then beyond Hari... There were corpses and corpses all along the pavement (165).

The graveyard—an indirect, but definite image of excrement—signifies 'ultimate waste.' Next morning, which is his first morning in Bombay, Munoo sets out, hoping for a job in the Cotton Mills. Walking along a sewage farm, he sees a "sunken pool of murky green water where crows wheeled over the pond in great profusion, pecking at the sores of the cows and bullocks." Not far away,

> On the plain cut into two by the parallel lines of a narrow-guage railway, were scattered rusty rails, heaps of dead coal, and all *the refuse which the factory emitted.* Under cover of these and of the *deep pits and puddles of mud into which the feet sank and stuck*, at little distances, sat *men relieving themselves.* And on the even surfaces, *fuel cakes of cow dung dried and festered with a stink that was unbearable* (170) (Emphasis added).

In other words, day breaks for Munoo with a vision of excrement and waste. A little later, on his way to the factory—that is his first day of work—Munoo, along with Hari and his family finishes his toilet most hurriedly:

> A second sharp, clear (factory) whistle hastened them before they had settled for very long.
>
> They arose and finished their toilets, sprinkling first their bottoms and then their faces with palmfuls of water from under the thick crusts of scum on the surface of the pond (182).

These passages are necessary to elucidate the nature of the ordering consciousness in Mulk Raj Anand's work. Munoo's grasp of his relation to the world around almost always is through his excremental sense.

A little later in the novel, on a ran-hit night, Hari's hut where Munoo also lives, is washed off and a co-worker Ratan provides them a place for that night. And again, the crisis of the situation is revealed to us through images relating to excrement. The immediate problem for Munoo is that of locating an appropriate place for completing his toilet. That happens to be a Sunday and Munoo is "awakened in the morning by the inrush into his nostrils by the most foul smell" (198). The toilet pipe of the house (where Munoo is sleeping) is broken and dirty water is overflowing into the gutter in the "crowded airless, stinking gully" which is "like a river of dung" (198). Ratan explains to Munoo that there "are seven latrines downstairs for two hundred men, and there is only one sweeper to clean the night soil away" (198). However, his friend Ratan asks him to go to a "special latrine" (by paying an anna) and avoid "communal latrine." Munoo cannot even bear the 'sight and smell' in the special latrine: "he was nauseated by the sight and smell of refuse in gutters, which passed for latrines... that he came out within a minute of his entrance" (199).

A blatant truth in Anand generally ignored by readers is his perception of the colonizer as capitalist landowner or mill-owner on vast territorial scales. After all, he possesses somebody else's land, extracting fully the native's labour. It is the excremental vision of Anand that makes the growth of Munoo's awareness of his lack of status in society correspond to his perception of the gulf between the white mill owners and native workers. In other words, the growth of a boy blends with the criticism of the social and political order mainly through images of excretion. Every manner of exploitation in Anand is exposed mostly through the excremental.

The poverty and the deprival of human status to workers is shown by Anand not so much in terms of food and clothing as in the desperate manner in which they look for a place to evacuate. It may be useful to recall, at this stage, E.M. Forster's "Preface" to *Untouchable.* He begins with an indignant colonel's comment that Forster had a 'dirty mind.' What vexed the colonel was this sentence in Forster's *A Passage to*

India: "The sweepers had just struck, and half the commodes of Chandrapore remained desolate in consequence." If that one sentence showed that the novelist had a 'dirty mind,' Forster wonders what that reader would have thought of *Untouchable*, which is full of references to excreta? "What a strange business man has been (sic) made of this business of the human body relieving itself" asks Forster and goes on, "the ancient Greeks did not worry about it, and they were the sanest and happiest of men. But both our civilization and the Indian civilization have got tied up in the most fantastic knots". One is impressed by Forster's comparison of civilizations on the basis of their attitudes to the excretal function. Forster attributes Anand's 'success' with *Untouchable* to the 'directness' with which the latter attacks the question of purity and pollution.

In *Untouchable* Bakha's attention is repeatedly drawn towards the waste of animals, birds and humans: "birds droppings" (49); "the litter of banyan leaves, flower petals, the droppings of the pigeons" (51); "A stray dog, thin, flea-bitten and diseased relieving itself" and "another dog licking at some decayed food on a refuse heap that lay blocking the drain" (57); "the little boy relieving in public" (63). The predicament of Bakha is rendered in terms of the image of the waste itself: "Because we touch dung they hate dung. I hate it too! That is why I came here. I was tired of working on the latrines every day" (45), reflects Bakha when he reviews the attitude of the Hindus towards the people who clear human excreta. He sums up the plight of the community of people who help dispose the waste products thus: "They think we are dirt because we clean their dirt" (68). In his comment on the excretal image in *Untouchable* Damodar Rao notes, "In a novel where the protagonist is a scavenger and where the major pre-occupation is with the system of untouchability, it is but natural that there should be repeated references to relieving" (70).

But it is important to see that "references to relieving" are not confined to *Untouchable*. The excremental or anal consciousness pervades Anand's works. Assessment or evaluation of character and evolution of socio-political systems is made in terms of this consciousness. Consider *The Village*. The attitude of village boys to city (city when seen as a making of the colonizer-culture) gets expressed through a reference to excretion. Lalu and his friends go to the town and as they approach it, Lalu warns his friends with good humoured contempt:

> 'It is the sacred hour of early morning'... 'come and mention the name of God and relieve yourselves... otherwise you get no occasion to do so in town' (97).

Lalu's predicament almost always gets expressed in terms of the excretal function. The following example may reinforce this point: When Lalu's regiment is given a call to get ready to go to 'vilayat,' his 'dreamland,' Lalu's response is one of elation and fear. Though elated at the prospect of seeing his wonderland, he fears that he may die there. His predicament is reflected through his urge for excretion:

> His heart beat pit-pat with the curious exaltation of joy to find himself actually on the way to vilayat as well as the fear that he might die fighting in the war to which they were all going. And he felt a motion in his belly. *He was sorry he hadn't been to the latrines before walking away from the barracks.* But the bank struck up and drowned the joy and the fear, as well as the urge for excretion (341) (Emphasis added).

Lalu is made aware of the subhuman status of the socially marginalized people like cobblers, weavers and Muhammadans of his village through the images of waste. For instance, Lalu and his friends decide on an escapade to the fair in the town and Lalu goes to pick up Ghulam, his Muhammadan friend. The appalling living conditions of this weaver boy are captured through images of excretion:

> It was a filthy room, cramped with a loom in the middle, an oven on one side and a huge bedstead on which the whole family slept on the other. *And sheep, hens and cocks revelled among their droppings all over the place reeking with several varieties of smell, and slimy with dirt* (76) (Emphasis added).

To an extent, Lalu in his early childhood had been conditioned by his mother's opinion that the Muhammadans were 'dirty.' But after seeing Ghulam's place he contemplates on the factor responsible for their dirtiness: "they were dirty, indeed, but they were the poorest people in the village" (76). Again, when he returns from town, Lalu approaches his house through the cobbler's lane instead of the main road. The villagers describe the inhuman atmosphere in which these untouchables dwell as "part of the kingdom of Yama in the hell" (125). As he walks towards the cobbler's lane, he slips into the drain and jumps

> into a ravine beyond which stood the sweepers' straw huts, winking with distended eyes at the village from which they *were segregated by the filthiest, most foully odorous pond from which the outcasts drew their water and where they and their cattle bathed.* The elders among the high castes told the children *that it was part of the kingdom of Yama in hell, to which it was connected by a subterranean darkness.*
>
> Lalu *lifted a lapel of his shirt to his nose and ran across the ramparts of dung excreted in the gorge by the lazy shopkeepers, who would not venture out into the fields to answer the call of nature* (124-125) (Emphasis added).

Not that Lalu was experiencing the smell of his village for the first time. In fact, as a child he had frequented this part of the village and felt this odour. But now it is "so repulsive" to his awakening consciousness. As in the case of Bakha and Munoo, Lalu grasps truths about the social and political worlds through his senses, which are very sensitive to excretory details. Consider his understanding of the locale of Ferozepur cantonment where he arrives as a sepoy. He compares and contrasts the sight of his own village with Ferozepur, and recognizes the difference between the two in terms of the odour of the dung:

> The beds of cowslips that yellowed a meadow at the foot of a red hill reminded him of the meadows where the cattle of his village grazed. Two crows cawing

> outside a confectioner's stall by the station reminded him of the swarms over the trees on his father's well. And there was the sun, the same... Even the lights and shades of the morning were the same...
>
> But no there was something different. The whiffs of horse-dung smell and the lines of barracks beyond that metalled road and a few orange-coloured bungalows by the side of more straight red barracks. And there was a uniformed angrezi soldier on guard with a rifle in his hand (239-40) (Emphasis added).

Talks and scenes of relieving are recurrent in the routine life of the regiment; Daddy Dhanoo, Lalu's elderly companion advises Lalu not to eat too much of the sweet he has gifted to him, as he may "get dysentery" (269). As long as he is in Ferozepur cantonment, Lalu regularly watches the soldiers "eternally walking away towards the latrines," holding "jugs in hand and whispering sacred verse" (276).

When Lalu returns to his own village Nandpur after a five-month stay in the regiment, the first important activity that is shown is his going to "fields with the boys to answer the call of nature as he used to do during the holidays" (295). The sight of cronies of his village relieving themselves together in the open becomes a cherishable episode to Lalu:

> 'Let us pay homage to the Almighty', said Gughi plunging into a millet field and sitting down to relieve himself.
>
> Churangi followed suit and could be heard loudly.
>
> 'Stuff yourself up with lentils a little more, you swine,' shouted Ghulam 'like father, like son. He belches wind in the shop all day as if his bottom were a big gun announcing the passing of each minute, and you will outdo him when you grow up. Why can't you at a little meat? You have piled up enough money.'

Lalu edged away, laughing at Ghulam's mocking outburst (296).

Churangi is an affluent merchant's son, whose anal habits are the surest indications of his class. Indeed, the anal consciousness is quite special in the evaluation of people and their attitudes. Another example from the novel illustrates further the primacy of this consciousness in Anand's world. On receiving a telegram that war had been declared Lalu returns to the regiment where some war-scared soldiers are busy devising stratagems to escape the war. One of the ways is to contract diarrhea:

> They wondered whether a bribe to the Head Clerk would get them exemption, or perhaps one to the Doctor Sahib at the hospital. The frequency with which men were issuing out of the barracks, jugs in hand, towards the public latrines indicated that the best plan was to buy a potion from the indigenous druggist in the cantonment bazaar in order to get dysentery (332).

Lalu however has no intention of avoiding the war, and he is found fit. As Lalu's ship sets sailing across the seas to the war front, he remembers his home village. His village becomes accessible to him through the excretal image:

> ... the village of Nandpur stood in the red glow of the morning sun, with the broker walls of its decrepit houses *pasted with cow-dung cakes* on which the crows pecked as they cawed (351) (Emphasis added).

Some readers feel that the cantonment section flaws the novel. C.J. George, for example, in Mulk Raj Anand: His Art and Concerns, says:

> The novel could have had sharper focus if the evocation of the village life had not been marred by the lengthy description of the life in the cantonment and the troop movement for the war. It is true that the hero of *The Village*, Lal Singh, is very much alive in the cantonment and is able to return in memory to his village and parents but that alone cannot satisfy the requirement of the title of the novel. Out of the 253 pages of the novel, 64 pages... deal exclusively with cantonment, quite away from the village (87).

The present discussion, it is hoped, will convince that *The Village* has 'sharp focus' because of Anand's excremental vision.

Not just the colonized land, but the European war situation as well as the absurdity and meaninglessness of World War I are rendered very powerfully through excretal images in *Across the Black Waters.* In this novel, Lalu who has enrolled himself as a sepoy in the British-Indian army goes to the European war front with many other poor young Indians to fight the Germans. If Lalu sees the whole of Europe in the right perspective it is because of his excremental vision. The continent has become a vast graveyard, a colossal drainage where the ultimate waste gets heaped up. Through one of Lalu's nightmares Anand captures the exact picture of the battlefield:

> The village was *festering with the dirty water,* which had been let loose by the demons to smother the fire, but in the foreground a great battle was raging between the hosts of Kali and the sepoys. And a multitude of dead was piling up, with contorted legs, blue nails, folder arms, bulging eyes and frothing angry mouths, men whose pain-racked faces spread a trembling dread and sorrow (136) (Emphasis added).

The traditional belief that crossing the sea is a sin appears to find justification as Lalu remembers his mother's description of different hells that sinners have to pass through. The description is closely connected with the image of 'waste':

> ... the hell where beings are cut, wounded and bruised by Yama and his hosts; the hell where reborn beings are struck down with blazing weapons, *severed into pieces and left to rot in the mud and the slime*; the hell where the sinners are crushed like sesum seeds; and *the hell where they have to swim through oceanic expanses of dirty drains* (172) (Emphasis added).

The conception of hell as an 'oceanic expanse of dirty water' figures as 'the river of dung' in *Coolie* and some other works. The reference could be to the terrible river *Vaitarinee* in Hindu Mythology. The river is ever in a spate of blood, filth and pus. The water-clogged trenches in *Across the Black Waters* corroborate too well the descriptions of the Hindu hell, which is construed as a cosmic drainage of dirty waters. The sepoys are compelled to remain in the dugouts, which are filled with muddy water due to incessant rains. Plagued by cold, hunger, insects and lice the sepoys trail through mud and marshes. They in fact "live in subterranean darkness" and are "transplanted into netherworld":

> They had already come through the long and weary trail and were now in the stage of waiting in this vast, timeless universe for their doom to fulfill itself as if they had been suddenly transplanted into the world of their ancestors where men struggled against the elements of Gods and destiny (*Across the Black Waters*, 152).

It is through these images of death, dirt and waste that the hell created by the colonizer's war becomes comprehensible to Lalu.

Without risking a psycho-analysis of Anand's character, one may speculate if the writer acquired this excremental vision in his early childhood. The autobiographical novel *Seven Summers* contains a revealing passage, describing Ram Chand (Lal Chand, Mulk Raj's father):

> He (father) was in the habit of relieving himself twice a day. And each time he went to the lavatory, he sat there at least for half an hour, reading the *Civil and Military Gazette* of the previous day which the post-orderly brought for him from the Officer's Mess, and also taking a primitive, instinctive delight in the act of excretion, in spite of the fact that he suffered from piles (*Seven Summers*, 65).

That was the father's indirect way of teaching his sons the value of time.

The genital consciousness in Ngugi's world corresponds to the excremental in Anand's. No attempt is made, it must be stated clearly, to equate the excremental with the genital. What is of interest in Anand and Ngugi is that the evaluation of social, political and cultural systems appear to be made mainly with reference to biological factors: excretion which is a bodily function and circumcision, which is bodily mutation. This evaluatory consciousness is conveniently termed 'excremental' or 'anal' in Anand, and 'genital' in Ngugi. A consciousness centred around the waist seems to operate as the ordering consciousness in quite a few novels by these writers. No doubt it is because of the centrality of this genital consciousness that the circumcision rite becomes conspicuous in many of Ngugi's works.

To the invasive Christian culture in Ngugi's world, circumcision is only a 'barbarous custom,' a 'brutal mutilation of the body' (*The River Between*, 56). From the natives' point of view however, circumcision is a determining factor in shaping Gikuyu psyche. Jomo Kenyatta's words may capture for us what the rite means to the Gikuyu:

> The real argument lies not in the defence of surgical operation or its details, but in the understanding of a very important fact in the psychology of Gikuyu—namely that this operation is still regarded as the very essence of an institution, which has enormous educational, social, moral and religious implications (*Facing Mount Kenya*, 133).

Circumcision (or *Irua*) in Gikuyu life symbolizes purity and unity of the tribe. It irrevocably forges the individual with the community and the land. This is the meaning of the blood the novice sheds during circumcision. Thus an individual, after undergoing circumcision is bound emotionally and morally to his / her community and to the land. After the rite, the claims of the tribe on the circumcised become greater than those of the family. Criticism of the practice of circumcision thus will be seen as a threat to community and land. Waiyaki in *The River Between* understands the importance of the rite thus:

> Circumcision was an important ritual to the tribe. It kept people together, bound the tribe. It was at the core of the social structure, and a something that gave meaning to a man's life. End the custom and the spiritual basis of the tribe's cohesion and integration would be no more (68).

Naturally the intensity of the conflict between whites and natives finds its most vehement expression over the issue of circumcision. The white man and his native ally, especially the convert, fail to comprehend the moral and spiritual significance of the circumcision rite and denounce it. They pledge themselves to end this practice. Muthoni's death after her circumcision results in Livingstone's banning admission in his school to children of the circumcised. Muthoni's Christian father Joshua disowns her once she rebels against Christianity's restriction in circumcision. Joshua joins Livingstone in the latter's determination to "root out the civil" (circumcision practice). He organizes camps and conducts Mass in an attempt to convert all the Gikuyus to the Christian faith. On the other hand true Gikuyus are as vehement as Christians. They determine to check Joshua's penetration into the interior Gikuyu region. For this purpose a Kiama—council of elders—is formed. The remark by a Gikuyu elder—"all the girls must be circumcised by force"—is a clear indication of the intensity of the conflicts. The whole land is divided over this issue: the white man (Livingstone) and his native section swear to end the practice; the natives take an oath to circumcise all the young, specially the girls. The circumcision issue becomes the most important factor in the Livingstone—Joshua alliance, but the natives see the custom as being inevitable for the unity of the tribe. For the 'true natives' circumcision becomes particularly urgent in the assertion of their culture and in the preservation of the tribe's purity and unity. "The issue which most clearly epitomizes the divisions in the (Gikuyu) society" (Palmer, 14) is Muthoni's circumcision.

The struggle between the practitioners of circumcision and its opponents gradually assumes a political dimension and the issue demands resolution at the political level. Ngugi's later novels reflect how a social custom like circumcision takes on a political tint. The Kiama is formed originally to protect the "purity and unity of the tribe;" to resist the white man's intrusion in the tribe's way of life. Later, the Kiama includes, as an item in its agenda the repossession of their ancestral lands and takes an 'oath' to redeem the country from the white man's menace. In other words, the Kiama, which started as a cultural forum transforms itself into a political organization. Some critics have pointed out the parallels between Kiama and Mau-Mau.[1]

Again, it is in terms of the attitude towards 'circumcision' that people engaged in the struggle are morally categorized. The circumcised ones are presented as 'true men,' 'patriots,' while those who resent or associate themselves with the opponents of circumcision (the black-white men) are seen as 'traitors' and enemies of the people. Kihika (in *A Grain of Wheat*), Abdulla (in *Petals of Blood*) and Matigari belong to the farmer category. They are all men who consider circumcision an inseparable aspect of their life. Mugo and Karanja in (*A Grain of Wheat*), Chui (in *Petals of Blood*) and Kihaahu Wa Gathica (in *Devil on the Cross*) who only think of circumcision as an expression of 'sensuality' or 'tribal frenzy' are shown as betrayers. Waiyaki's people in *The River Between* consider him a betrayer because of his association with Nyambura, an uncircumcised girl. Waiyaki himself understands the meaning of his contact with an uncircumcised girl as he recalls his mother's reaction: "In her eyes such a relationship with a girl who was not circumcised would be a betrayal" (*The River Between*, 20).

An episode (relating to the issue of circumcision) in the early life of Kihika—the real hero of Mau-Mau in *A Grain of Wheat* demonstrates the conflict of values between natives and outsiders, but more importantly it reveals how a 'patriot' emerges out of such a clash. Kihika, a young pupil in the Mission School, objects to the missionary-teacher's explanation that circumcision is a "heathen practice," a "sinful act" and hence "all the Christians are forbidden to carry on such practices" (99). He insists that the teacher provide supportive evidence from the Bible (since he had read the Bible repeatedly) but the teacher fails to provide one. Defeated, the teacher reports the matter to the school authorities who try to punish Kihika for his "irreverence." Rather than accept the unjust punishment, Kihika—"little hero" in the eyes of the native pupils—leaves the school that instant and emerges, later, as a hero of Mau-Mau, the patriotic struggle against the colonial regime. Through a small but significant event in the life of a young boy, Ngugi enacts the birth of a patriot. Circumcision becomes synonymous with patriotism. Consider for instance how Abdulla, one of the protagonists of *Petals of Blood* recounts to his people the aspirations with which he joined Mau-Mau; how he became a truly "circumcised" man in order to

> Redeem the land: to fight so that the industries like the shoes factory, which had swallowed his sweat could belong to people: So that the children could one day have enough to eat and to wear under adequate shelter from rain: So that they would say in pride, my father died that I might live: this had transformed him from a *slave* before a boss into a man. *That was the day of his true circumcision into a man* (136) (Emphasis added).

The equation between circumcision and patriotism is also worked out in the ending of *Matigari.* The hero here tries to reach the Mugumo tree across the river to recover the arms he had buried under it:

> The dogs leaped on Matigari and Guthera. They crowded around them. They tore their clothes, their flesh... Their blood mingled and it trickled into the soil, on the bank of the river (173).

This is a symbolic enactment of the circumcision rite. The blood of Matigari—"the patriot who survived the bullets" (124)—irrevocably binds him to the land he loved. The patriots are associated with circumcision, the traitors are totally disassociated from it. The natives resent any reference from the traitors to circumcision. The following example brings out this resentment. In *A Grain of Wheat,* Karanja, John Thompson's (white man's) office boy—the black-white character—abuses his co-worker Mwara for entering the office without knocking on the door louder: "why can't you knock hard, hard like a circumcised man?" Irritated by the reference to circumcision by a blackman who looks at the blackmen and their ways as a white man does, Mwara reacts to Karanja; "Ask your mother... ask your sister. It is they who can tell you Mwara is a man circumcised" (63). Native elites (Chui in

Petals of Blood, Gathica in *Devil on the Cross* (119, 124)) like their European counterparts, perceive the circumcision ritual—its songs and dances—as a manifestation of 'sensuality,' "the tribal frenzy." The entire 'uhuru' (Independence Day) celebrations (in *A Grain of Wheat*) turns out to be a circumcision-like ceremony: songs and dance are part of the celebration. The people welcome the freedom fighters in the way they "welcome a son at birth or circumcision" by calling "the five Ngeme" (232).[2]

A convenient approach to the excremental and the genital in Anand and Ngugi becomes available in the study of the boy-girl relationship. Young boys like Lalu (in *The Village, Across the Black Waters,* and *The Sword and the Sickle*), Bikhu (in *The Road*), Bakha (in *Untouchable*), Waiyaki (in *The River Between*), and Njoroge (in *Weep Not, Child*) are troubled by conflicting loyalties and demands, as shown in the previous chapter. The conflicts get compounded when these boys get attracted to girls like Maya (in 'Lalu' Trilogy), Rukmani (in *The Road*), Ram Charan's sister (in *Untouchable*), Nyambura (in *The River Between*), Mwihaki (in *Weep Not, Child*) who belong to oppositional families. Either because of the right caste system (as in *Untouchable* and *The Road*) or because of alignment with the European ruler (as in *Weep Not, Child* and *The River Between*), the closer the boy and the girl aspire to be, the farther their families drift away from each other. Shades of classical love-stories like *Romeo and Juliet, Heer Ranjha* and *Radha-Krishna* can be seen in the rendering of these relationships. But that is not the point. The point is that the nature of impediments to the relationship between boy and girl is communicated to us through the 'excremental' or the 'genital.' We may briefly consider how the oppressive nature of the social system is revealed through the excretal images in Lalu's case. In *The Village* young Lalu is attracted to Maya, landlord Harbans Singh's daughter. The landlord who is hostile to Lalu's family is displeased by Lalu-Maya friendship. He fabricates criminal charges against Lalu who flees the village to enlist himself in the British-Indian army. That is the only way Lalu can escape the police. Transported to Flanders, he fights against the Germans in *Across the Black Waters*, entertaining hopes of receiving a little land from the English masters as reward for the military services he renders. Returning to his village in the third part of the Trilogy, *The Sword and the Sickle*, Lalu finds that Maya is married and widowed almost simultaneously. Love between Lalu and Maya is as alive as it was. Clandestine meetings between the lovers take place in spite of the constant watch the servants keep over her (since she is the landlord's daughter). Maya is able to effect an escape from her house under cover of darkness, in the pretext of attending nature's call. "I slipped out on the excuse of going to fields" (70), she informs Lalu. It is interesting to note that the time most appropriate for the meeting of the lovers is the toilet hour. Likewise her departure from Lalu's place is well-timed:

> Lalu sat on into the morning after Maya had gone, timing her departure to the hour when women went to and from the field to compelte their toilet under cover of the dark before men (71).

Otherwise stated, the private meeting between the lovers takes place with the excretal activity of the village ruling the consciousness of Lalu and Maya.

A similar example from *Untouchable* could be cited. Bakha, who is attracted to Ram Charan's sister, recollects a time when he was aroused by her picture:

> Then from the dark undeclared places of his soul arose another picture of her in his memory—as she came through the darkness before the dawn from the banks of the brook where, he knew, she and the other women of the outcastes' colony went every day, taking advantage of the privacy which the half-light afforded, to perform their toilets unseen by men. He remembered that he had been about the latrines and had at first felt a thrill of delight, then a sensation more vital... An impulse had arisen in his spine, and darkened his thoughts. He had felt as if he could forcibly gather the girl in his embrace and ravish her (75).

Almost analogous to the anal-factor is the circumcision-factor in Ngugi, as evident for example in *The River Between.* Waiyaki meets Nyambura, the girl he is in love with. A depressed Nyambura has sought her favourite spot on the bank of the river Honia. That place is adjacent to the "circumcision-spot." Waiyaki watches her from the other bank:

> A pleasurable numbness dulled Waiyaki into immobility. He did not move but leaned against a tree and watched the apparition. The girl was on the opposite bank, in a flat clearing hidden a little by small bushes. Waiyaki could not tell why the place reminded him so much of the sacred grove where long ago his father had taken him and revealed the ancient prophecy. This place she was in was sacred too... A kind of holy light seemed to emanate from her body. The place would for ever remain sacred to him. *A few yards away from here was the place where he had sat long ago when being circumcised. It was the place where he had shed blood,...*
>
> Their eyes met and they did not utter a word. Nyambura was afraid of the intense excitement that possessed her. Then Waiyaki made as if to move again...
>
> 'Don't run away, Teacher,' she said.
>
> A pleasant shock went through Waiyaki and made his body hot with desire (104-5) (Emphasis added).

The genital in Ngugi parallels the excremental in Anand. This consciousness works by integrating society with the interactions between individuals. It is through the anal and the genital that we see the private drama related to the political, social and cultural drama.

One cannot forget that for Anand and Ngugi who are writers belonging to agrarian countries, organic communities are readily available for fictional purposes; that an organic community is still an Indian reality or an African reality. The 'anal' and the 'genital' respectively in Anand and Ngugi help to making the organic community fictionally reachable. The circumcision of Muthoni in *The River Between* is in this context certainly interesting. It is during this ceremony that Waiyaki, who (because of long absences from the hills) "had been out of touch, with those things that mattered most to the tribe" (39), can give himself up to the rhythm of the tribe:

> The dance was being held at an open-air place in Kameno. Whistles, horns, broken tins and anything that was handy were taken and beaten into the rhythm of the song and dance... Old and young, women and children, all were there loosing themselves in the magic motion of the dance... They were free... Age and youth had been reconciled for this one night... Somebody pulled him (Waiyaki) into the circle... And suddenly he felt as if a hand soft and strong had held his soul and whipped it off (40-42).

The suggestion of the organic nature of the community is dexterous indeed: "Whistles, broken tins, anything that was handy was beaten to the rhythm of the song and dance." Like the others, Waiyaki is baffled by Muthoni's rebellion against her Christian father and asks her why she underwent circumcision. Muthoni replies in a voice that is "clean" but "vibrant with sadness":

> I say I am a Christian and my father and mother have followed the new faith. I have not run away from that. But I also want to be initiated into the ways of the tribe... I knew that my father would not let me and so I came... I want to be a woman. How could I be outside the tribe, when all the girls born with me at the same time have left me? (43-44).

Waiyaki is "carried away" by her vibrant voice, as she continues: "I want to be a woman made beautiful in the tribe; a husband for my bed; children to play around the hearth" (44). Muthoni has returned to the tribe's faith.

In the light of Muthoni's action, Waiyaki understands that Livingstone is biased against the practice of circumcision. He knows now that Livingstone "did not understand and probably would never understand" the real significance of this custom to a 'proper Gikuyu.' The value of circumcision does not lie merely in its being a puberty rite which enables an individual to seek entry into the world of adults but in the prospect of becoming an institution ensuring the unity of the tribe. "The moral code" of the tribe, as Kenyatta says is connected with this rite; "it symbolizes the unification of the whole tribal organization" (*Facing Mount Kenya*, 134). Muthoni's death after circumcision and the Livingstone-Joshua policy to "root out" the practice of circumcision sharpen the conflicts in the Gikuyu region. Towards the end of the novel Waiyaki realizes the need to be a part of his people's tradition. He regrets isolating himself from native culture:

> He wished he would have taken a more active part in the ceremonial activities of the tribe. That, at least, would have given him more comfort and made him feel still one of the people (121).

While it is true that circumcision is treated in great detail in The River Between, references to ritual are not limited to that one text. For instance, allusions to circumcision appear to be 'casual' in *Weep Not, Child* but are quite important to understand its meaning. There is a subtle, significant contrast made between Njoroge and his brother Kamau. This brother with whom Njoroge is quite intimate, functions subtly as a moral arbiter. Curiously this character has not received due attention, even from G.D. Killam, who offers detailed and perceptive analyses of Ngugi's works. It is Kamau who keeps informing Njoroge of the changing situation in the world outside Njoroge's school. From his early childhood Kamau works as an apprentice to a carpenter. Why does he not go to school, asks the school-going Njoroge, once. Kamau is firm that he will not. He displays a maturity beyond his years when he replies, "A man without land must learn to trade. Father has nothing. So what I am doing is important" (38). His attitude to education also appears to be correct (irrespective of whether the educated Njoroge testifies to this or not): "Your learning is for all. Father says the same thing. He is anxious that you go on, so you might bring light to our home. Education is the light of Kenya" (38). From his very early life Kamau values only what is good for all. When Kamau grows up to be ready for circumcision, Njoroge watches him with fear:

> When Kamau was initiated, he would probably walk with men of his *Rika* (age group). But this was not what he feared... What he feared was that one day Kamau might be drawn into the city. The other brothers had been called. Though they came home quite regularly, they are changing... Kamau's going would lead to a final family break-up and ruin the cosy security, which one felt when thinking of home. He seemed to carry the family dumbly on his shoulders (48).

The most striking thing about Kamau is his ability to make moral choices. When there is a letter (purportedly by the dreaded Mau-Mau) threatening to kill the headmaster and the students of the school run by whites, Njoroge's mother asks Njoroge to stop going to school. "Education is not life" she says. "I thought Mau-Mau was on the side of the black people," cries an offended Njoroge. The most balanced person is Kamau whose voice is persuasive:

> You'll be foolish to leave school. The letter may not be genuine. Besides, do you really think you'll be safer at home? I tell you there is no safety anywhere. There's no hiding in this naked land (83).

Above all, Kamau's importance lies in his being a moral arbiter. This is clearly seen in an episode where Njoroge seeks clarification from Kamau, relating to the strike against the white settlers in which Ngotho, their father is to participate. Ngotho is reduced to a squatter on his ancestral lands, now owned by Howlands:

> Njoroge remembered something he had wanted to ask about land.
>
> 'Do you think it's true what father says, that all the land belongs to black people?' (Njoroge).
>
> 'Yes. Black people have their land in the country of black people. White men have their land in their own country. It is simple. I think it was God's plan' (Kamau).

> 'Are there black people in England?'
>
> 'No England is for white people only.'
>
> 'And they all left their country to come and rob us acres of what we have?'
>
> 'Yes. They are robbers.'
>
> 'All of them?'
>
> 'Yes. Even Mr Howlands.'
>
> 'Mr Howlands... I don't like him. I did not like the way his son followed me once.'
>
> 'A lamb takes after its mother' (43).

Kamau's tone in this passage is representative of his voice throughout. It is dispassionate, without bitterness or anger; balanced.

The purpose of this discussion of Kamau is to focus on his poise, which reflects his father's and derives from his concern for home: "It was he who kept the home together, buying food, clothes and paying fees for Njoroge" (84). And in the patriarchical Gikuyu tribe, this stature is possibly only after circumcision. A very important duty Kamau has undertaken is that of bearing the circumcision costs of Njoroge. It is in his adolescence that Njoroge feels "the full force of the chaos that had come over the land" (84). This is the time when has to be circumcised, and Kamau meets the cost since the other brothers are not at home.

Considering these factors, it may be assumed that the circumcision-factor indicates an ordering consciousness in *Weep Not, Child.* But one needs to consider *Petals of Blood* in order to see the way the genital consciousness organizes the substance of the novel.

Bulkier than *A Grain of Wheat, The River Between* and *Weep Not, Child, Petals of Blood* is divided into four parts with four protagonists—Abdulla, Karega, Munira and Wanja. The narrative technique varies from omniscient narration to the first person 'I' and 'we.' In addition to the shifts in the narration, there are time-shifts from past to present and *vice-versa.* What moulds these various strands of narration into one work is the circumcision-factor.

Circumcision most prominently figures as a key to past—both personal and historical—in *Petals of Blood.* And, re-enactment of the past appears to be Ngugi's major preoccupation in this novel. All the central characters are obsessed with the past—"of a past. A great past. A past when Ilmorog, or all Africa, controlled its own earth" (125). Karega expresses the modern spirit when he tells Wanja—"To understand the present... You must understand the past. To know where you are, you must know where you came from" (127-28). Its significance also can be seen in the fact that much of the novel's setting is in Ilmorog—an ancient place; and all the four protagonists find themselves in Ilmorog. The past of the protagonists along with the pastness of the land, begins to unfold itself most succiently with reference to circumcision. The first serious allusion to circumcision occurs in the book when the Ilmorog people go on a journey to Nairobi. The group halts for a brief rest by a solitary hill. It is a moonlight night, and Karega, looking at the hill, wonders: "Isn't it strange that hill should have stood when all else collapsed?" Indeed there is a special meaning in the hill still standing when all else has collapsed. That hill is called 'the hill of the circumcised boys' (126), replied Wanja. There are stories about the hill, that a boy will turn into a girl and a girl into a boy when one runs right round the hill. As Karega falls into a reverie, this hill relates him to "another hill in another plain" (127)—Manguo marshes (also connected with circumcision)—where he used to meet his girl Mukami. His past begins to unfold itself to him as he starts gazing at the hill.

But the startling blend of the different narrative sections takes place after the circumcision ceremony, which follows a harvest. Munira is able to reclaim his past through the Ilmorog circumcision ceremony:

> As a boy Munira used to hide from home to listen to the singing, which accompanied the ceremony. And even as a young teacher, after Siriana, he once or twice stole to the ceremonies. That was before the dances were

> banned during the Emergency. It was during one of the ceremonies that he had met Julia. She was then Wanjiru. Her voice, her dancing, her total involvement had attracted him and he had decided that here at last was what would bring fulfilment to his life. But she had become Julia and the temporary dream of an escape into sensuality had vanished on the marriage bed (203).

A son of a pious Christian father, Munira had undergone circumcision stealthily in a hospital, under the effect of a pain-killer. His undergoing the circumcision in an 'irregular' way has always made him feel "a little incomplete." He is bothered by the feeling of not belonging to his "age group: Gicia Banje" (204). Munira's love of circumcision songs and dances further indicates his desire to relate himself to people and land through the ancient practice. Karega's fascination for the circumcision ritual too is obvious:

> Karega could hardly wait for Saturday. He had always liked the dances connected with the ritual of circumcision and the singing, especially when two or more good singers happened to be present and faced one another in a kind of poetry contest. Then his heart would be lifted to lands far and beautiful where people held together by a common spirit (206-7).

During the ceremony, the Ilmorog elders Nyakinyua and Njuguna relate to the newly circumcised youth the story of Kenya's struggle against the foreign invasions. This is a ritual where the past is re-enacted so as to make it a community-sharing. And the private pasts of individuals get linked to the community's past. There is a feeling of togetherness and happiness in the participants.

A unique feature of the ceremony is the 'Theng'eta drink' made out of a "mysterious" small plant with "four tiny red petals" (210). And this is a 'spirit' taken only after ceremonies like circumcision, marriage or Ituika[3] (205). Strange powers are attributed to Theng'eta: it can remove woman's barrenness and can increase man's potency. It is a central symbol in the text. Eager for this drink, the four protagonists with other participants, sit in a circle. Old Nyakinyua, the mother-figure of Ilmorog, who has brewed the drink for the occasion, explains the significance of circumcision practice:

> They came... later in the evening. Under the mood of the frank atmosphere of the circumcision ceremony, they all felt together—a community sharing a secret. They sat in circle according to their ages. Munira found himself sitting next to Njuguna. Wanja sat between Abdulla and Karega. They all removed their ties, their shoes, anything which might prevent their bodies from being loose and at ease. She (Nyakinyua) commanded them to remove all the money in the pockets, the metal bug that split up homes and drove men to city. She took all the money and put it away on the floor outside the ritual circle. She sat down (211).

And cheered "Millet, Power of God."

Under the effect of Theng'eta each protagonist unites the knot of his/her tale. And, they discover that each one is related to the others in the past. Nyakinyua—"the link binding past, present and future"—is the main speaker. Her tale about her husband's heroic struggle against white man, her reference to Abdulla's 'stump of leg,' are also events, which relate them to past. Karega goes down his memory lane and begins his narration cheering. 'Millet, Power of God!' His narration reveals that his mother Miriamu was a labourer on Munira's father's land and his brother had been a Mau-Mau fighter along with Abdulla. The narration of his association with Munira's sister Mukami (who commits suicide later) gives a twist to the novel's development. The significance of Karega's narration is that it reveals his personal past, historical past and also the mythical past. Karega recalls the 'spot' where he and Mukami used to meet. And this again is in some way connected to circumcision:

> In the middle of Manguo lake were two humps, which were never covered by water no matter how it rained, they always seemed to float above water. Later I learnt that these were sides of a dam built by the young men

> of Kihiu Mwiri generation at the insistence of Mukoma Wa Njiriri, then a chief, as a condition of giving them *license for initiation.* But... legend among us boys had it that they were the humps of two giant shark-like animals that used to dwell in the lake, and the needs were supposed to be their *puberty hair* (218) (Emphasis added).

The mythical past is thus invoked with reference to initiation. Karega's tale also informs us about the historical past. The failure of marriage between Karega and Mukami is because of the historical past. Karega's brother, Ndinguri, who was a Mau-Mau, had cut off Mukami's father's right ear as a warning for his allegiance to white ruler. Because of this, Mukami had informed Karega that (her father) would "never let his daughter marry into such a family, so poor and with such a history of crime" (219). Karega's story generates in Munira a hatred for the former. Munira holds Karega responsible for the death of his sister Mukami. We also learn that Karega's brother was Abdulla's childhood friend. The story invokes Abdulla's past and he begins his narration cheering, 'Millet, Power of God!' His story is in effect the story of colonial Kenya. Thus, Theng'eta spirit reveals that all the otherwise unrelated character were connected to one another in some way or the other in the past. Individual stories of the four characters blend into one.

The circumcision image helps Ngugi to organize his fictional material in other way too. In *The River Between* Waiyaki, the central character is introduced alongside references to circumcision. When the central female characters Muthoni and Nyambura are introduced, their thoughts concern circumcision (beginning of Chapter 6). The novel *Matigari* is in a way, framed by references to circumcision at the beginning and at the end of the book:

> The water had numbed their skin, so that none of them felt the pain as the knife cut into the flesh. Before this moment, they were mere boys, but by the time they unclenched their fists, they were men. Their blood

> mingled with the soil, and they became patriots, ready for the armed struggle to come (4).
>
> The dogs leaped on Matigari and Guthera. They crowded around them. They tore at their clothes, their flesh. But not once, not once did Matigari let go of Guthera. Their blood mingled and it trickled into the soil, on the banks of the river (173).

Likewise, the references to excretion frame Untouchable and The Village. "Rakha and Sohini will still be asleep when I go to latrines" (12) ruminates Bakha at the opening of *Untouchable* and the narrative ends with his question "But shall I never be able to leave the latrines?" (132).

But above everything, the genital and the excremental make possible visionary ability. How can Christian truth, for example, be banned to a native who is circumcised? Muthoni tells a father-fearing sister Nyambura:

> Father and mother are circumcised. Are they not Christian? Circumcision did not prevent them from being Christians. I too have embraced the white man's faith. However, I know it is beautiful, oh so beautiful to be initiated into womanhood. You learn the ways of the tribe. Yes, the white man's God does not quite satisfy me. I want, I need something more. My life and your life are here, in the hills, that you and I know (*The River Between*, 26).

Muthoni dies, uttering peacefully,

> 'Waiyaki... tell Nyambura I see Jesus. And I am a woman made beautiful in the tribe' (53).

It is as if Muthoni's stature is elevated to a seer's after her circumcision.

The visionary element in Anand's novel too seems to derive from the excremental. Any experience of a new land, locale is made through the excremental. When Lalu goes to France, he experiences the difference between his land and France in the way he regards the rain there: "Their rain is like the pissing of the child" (33). Lalu's realization of the common humanity of mankind is also through the anal consciousness:

> ...the Hindustanis were a separate nation like the Germans and the Francisis and the Angrezi people! And they deserved respect as men. Why should they always be abused by the Goras as blackmen who were used to relieving themselves on the ground! In the war he had seen the Goras do the same. They had the right to be a separate nation and, what was more, they had the right to own their land! (*The Sword and the Sickle*, 83).

Again, one may consider how different places reveal themselves to Munoo in *Coolie.* After the first incident in Sham Nagar, which quickened his consciousness Munoo begins to perceive every new environment, every new journey with reference to human and animal waste. The novel in five sections deals with four journeys to different parts of the Indian sub-continent: from Bilaspur to Sham Nagar; and to Daulatpur; from there to Bombay; then to Simla. And finally from life to death itself. Each journey, each new place is seen by Munoo through the reference to excretal activity. We have already seen in detail Munoo's first experience in Sham Nagar. Similarly, while travelling from Daulatpur (where his life was happy for a brief period) to Bombay, Munoo wakes up at Delhi Central Station where the train stops for a while and hurries to "relieve himself by a water-pump among the intersecting railway lines. Then he came back and lay down for a second sleep" (146). The first thing he notices on his arrival in Bombay—"strange, hybrid, complex cosmopolitan Bombay"—apart from the towering buildings is a crow sitting on the Victoria Statue and relieving itself. After "emerging from a Victoria Station" Munoo walks along the street and finally finds a place to sit on a bench at the foot of the statue:

> Oppressed and overcast, the boy walked along the square wiping streams of sweat off his face, till he sighted a bench at the foot of a marble statue of the short, stocky, broad-bottomed Victoria with a scroll in her hands and a crown on her head, on which a *blue-black crow* cawed defiance to the world as it danced and fluttered after relieving itself (153).

Through such images of the waste, Anand captures the workers' world as one that is not lift for human habitation. Munoo perceives every new environment which is, in effect, more dehumanizing than the previous ones in terms of the excretal function. Not only is the awareness of the 'human world' guided by anal activity but his understanding of the cosmic world, the creation of the landscape, is generated in terms of the excretal function. That applies to Munoo's perception of the mountains of Simla where he arrives in the closing section of the novel. The mountains intimately connect him to his own village as if "it was only yesterday that he had left the village in the valley":

> The endless lengths of the mountains, the far, far stretches of sky-high peaks covered with snow, the colossal solidity of their shapeless masses, aroused in him the feeling, which he always used to have in his childhood, the urge to say what a great fool God was that when he came to relieve himself he excreted mountains and mountains and mountains, and that when he came to 'make water' he poured down vast, vast, vast sheets of rivers... (256).

These examples sufficiently explain how man's interaction and conflicts with his environment is guided by the 'anal' in Anand and the 'genital' in Ngugi.

One final observation before the conclusion of the chapter. The anal consciousness in Anand appears to be accentuated in novels where young boys are made central. Where adolescents are not heroes, there appears to be an abatement in the images of excretion. Instead, images of death seem to take over. Gangu the hero of *Two Leaves and a Bud* is a middle-aged coolie who has a fifteen-year old daughter and a nine-year old son. In rendering the experiences of Gangu or in ordering the world in that novel, Anand does not employ excretal images. However, there are, quite in abundance, images of death. The novel is about the impossible life-conditions of coolies in the tea estate of Assam where Englishmen are estate-owners and even moneylenders. The equation between capitalist and colonizer, coolie and colonized is more direct in this novel than in *Coolie.* Malaria and Cholera are constant companions of the coolies in the estates. In fact, Gangu contracts Malaria soon after arriving (from his native Punjab) in the estate. He is lucky to survive, not so his wife. Death—images in this work keep glaring at the reader. The picture of Sajani dying away in Gangu's arm is a moving one:

> ... as he crouched woodenly by the dead body, he looked at her again. In the violent struggle of her will against Yama, her even, round face had lengthened to the extreme limits of its contour, so that her open mouth disclosed the decayed teeth with a yellow film, protruding out of their purple guns. This was not the face, which Gangu had always known, eager with all the living impulses. It was haggard and worn and the blue veins under its transparent flesh were discoloured a ghastly green. Gangu had her body, but the tingling warmth of her passionate embrace seemed so distant now. He tried to touch her but he could not. In a flash, he seemed to comprehend the tragedy not only of his sex, but the significance of that ugly fact, which started him in the face—death (107-8).

An interesting image that communicates the pervasiveness of death in the novel is that of cholera:

> The fear of death by cholera had scared some of the coolies of the low-lying plantations, and recruiting was becoming more difficult in the plains...
>
> The water supply was at fault. It was the main source from which the disease spread. And it was criminal not to do anything about it. All the gardens in the area drew their water supply from wells,... and all these sources were unsatisfactory (18).

In the choleric condition, it need not be made obvious, excrements are excessive to a fatal degree.

Death, to repeat, is ultimate waste, and death-image appears to be an extension of the excretal. A prominent feature of the Lalu Trilogy is growing affiliation between images of excretion and images of death. In *The Village* where

Lalu is very young, images of evacuation are not abundant. In Across the Black Waters the graveyard image occurs alongside images of drainage, and Hell gets described as oceanic waste. In *The Sword and the Sickle* there is a greater alignment taking place between the images of death and images of waste. Lalu in this novel is not too young, one must remember. He has seen other lands and wars. Returning from the war front, as he is about to enter his village, Lalu receives the shocking news that his mother died two years ago. Standing at the edge of the village, he regards the cremation ground and the murky parts of the village, simultaneously:

> For a moment he stopped and lifted his head towards the groves, visible beyond the cremation ground by the monastery, but at the thought that both his father and mother must have been burnt there, and their spirits, turned malignant and angry at his neglect, would be flying to possess him, he resumed his steps.
>
> Two weaver women sat combing wool on big combs at their doorsteps and looked at his strange hurrying figure inquisitively. He hung his head down as he recognized one of them who used to earn a copper by making dung cakes for his mother.
>
> Further ahead, the crumbling earth of his old friend Ghulam's house lay mouldering in the putrid scum of the irregular drain. He felt the gulf between himself and his village widening, as if he were looking at it from far away (42).

An important section of the novel is about the involvement of Lalu and his companions with forced labourers in the Nasaribad estate. In this part, Chandra, a sick labourer is flogged out from bed to work and the boy collapses while cutting wood and dies. Lalu suggests that they carry the dead body in a procession to Allahabad in order to make the national leaders become aware of the brutality of landlords. The manager of the estate fires at the procession and a bullet hits one of Lalu's 'comrades,' Nandu. Once again images of death and waste coincide:

> Conscious of his responsibility for the misadventures into which he had led them. Lalu bent down and strained to lever the dead bodies with trembling hands. A sharp odour of decomposing flesh shot up to his nostrils from Chandra's body, while his hands were smeared with blood from Nandu's neck. He sat up imagining the smell to be a whiff of the foul virulence of bacterial decay, ensuing from the vegetation of the forest through which they had come. But, as he bent down again, there was no disguising the stink of the corpse. And, in a flash he realized that though Nandu's blood was hot now, it would soon be cold and the body would stink if it was carried all the way to Allahabad (181-82).

Lalu similarly regards the death of another companion, the old peasant Bhupendra. The passage, despite its length, is worth quoting:

> Lalu thought again and again of the brevity and senselessness of life, as he walked into Rajgarh, of how the old man had been alive and working only a little while ago, and how a mere push had killed him... he turned away, with ever-increasing irritation, from the dust of the footpath, which connected the village to the metalled road, and hurried by the cottage hospital and the manure dumps. He felt he was being chased by all the putrefying smells, as if he were being stung by each dry stalk of bush and grass in the dhak forest, which encroached upon the village.
>
> A wisp of hot wind blew to his face from the corner of Humble Lane... Above the far-distant curve of the earth beyond the Ganga, he could see a whirlwind arise, dark and menacing, and, through all the superstitions he had imbibed in his childhood, each grain of rolling sand seemed like a jinn or a bhut, (ghost) the harbinger of a death-storm.
>
> Some crows flew over, caw-cawing, wheeled and dived for shelter in the niches of the Rajgarh temple. And,

> before Lalu had entered the courtyard of the palace, the dust-storm had advanced over the cremation ground on the riverside, as if gathering all the spirits of the dead who were coming to welcome old Bhupendra to themselves, and the land was enveloped deep in sand and dust (237-38).

The equation between waste and death is most emphatic in *The Sword and the Sickle* where the hero is not too young, say like Lalu in *The Village* or Bakha in *Untouchable* or Munoo in *Coolie.*

NOTES

1. Ian Glenn finds significant resemblances between Kiama and Mau-Mau as seen in some of their activities like the burning of Christian huts, oath taking and the demand for land. And, the protagonist's (Waiyaki's) ambivalent attitude to Kiama is very much like Jomo Kenyata's to Mau-Mau. See his essay "Ngugi Wa Thiong'o and the dilemma of the intellectual elite in Africa: A Sociological Perspective." English in Africa, 8.2 (1981) 53-66.

   David Maughan-Brown is also of the view that "Ngugi had Mau-Mau in mind" when he wrote about the Kiama in *The River Between.* See his essay "Four Sons of One Father: A Comparison of Ngugi's Earliest Novels with works by Mwangi, Mangua and Wachira." *Research in African Literature* 16.2 (1981) 179-209. These observations are interesting; *The River Between* is set in the beginning of the colonial occupation when the Mau-Mau had not yet started. Ngugi's treatment of Kiama shows his own ambiguous attitude towards Mau-Mau in the early years of his career.
2. "Thrilling sounds uttered by women in applause." See Glossary. *Facing Mount Kenya.* By Jomo Kenyatta. 1938. Nairobi: East African Educational Publishers (1992) 326.
3. Refers to a "peaceful revolution in which one generation takes over the government from the preceding one" in Gikuyu legend.

WORKS CITED

Anand, Mulk Raj. *Across the Black Waters,* 1940. Bombay: Popular—Kutub, 1955.

Anand, Mulk Raj. *Coolie.* 1936. New Delhi: Penguin, 1993.

Anand, Mulk Raj. *Seven Summers.* 1951. New Delhi: Arnold-Heinemann, 1987.

Anand, Mulk Raj. *The Road.* 1961. New Delhi: Sterling Publishers, 1987.

Anand, Mulk Raj. *The Sword and the Sickle.* 1942. New Delhi: Arnold-Heinemann, 1984.

Anand, Mulk Raj. *The Village.* London: Jonathan Cape, 1939.

Anand, Mulk Raj. *Two Leaves and a Bud.* 1937. New Delhi: Arnold Associates, 1994.

Anand, Mulk Raj. *Untouchable.* 1935. Mysore: Geetha Book House, 1995.

Forster, E.M. Preface. *Untouchable.* By Mulk Raj Anand. 1935. Mysore: Geetha Book House, 1995.

George, C.J. *Mulk Raj Anand: His Art and Concerns.* New Delhi: Atlantic Publishers, 1994.

Kenyatta, Jomo. *Facing Mount Kenya.* 1938. Nairobi: East African Educational Publications, 1992.

Killam, G.D. *An Introduction to the Writings of Ngugi.* London: Heinemann, 1972.

Niven, Alastair. *The Yoke of Pity: A Study in the Fictional Writings of Mulk Raj Anand.* New Delhi: Arnold-Heinemann, 1978.

Palmer, Eustace. *An Introduction to the African Novel.* London: Heinemann, 1972.

Rao, Damodar. Afterwood. *Untouchable.* By Mulk Raj Anand. Mysore: Geetha Book House, 1995.

Rao, Damodar. "Social and Political Awareness in the Novels of the Mulk Raj Anand and George Orwell." Diss. U of Mysore, 1979.

Thiong'o, Ngugi wa. *A Grain of Wheat.* 1967. London: Heinemann, 1974.

Thiong'o, Ngugi wa. *Devil on the Cross.* (First published in Gikuyu, 1980). London: Heinemann, 1982.

Thiong'o, Ngugi wa. *Matigari.* (First published in Gikuyu, 1987). Nairobi: East African Educational Publishers, rpt. 1994.

Thiong'o, Ngugi wa. *Petals of Blood.* 1977. London: Heinemann, 1978.

Thiong'o, Ngugi wa. *The River Between.* 1965. London: Heinemann, 1985.

Thiong'o, Ngugi wa. *Weep Not, Child.* 1964. London: Heinemann, 1985.

Naked Land

4

Land is perhaps one of man's most urgent physical and spiritual needs. The bitterest of battles between peoples are fought over land and territory. Man's noblest aspirations and his fundamental feelings like desire, fear, greed and envy seek to express themselves potentially through the image of land. This may partly explain: (a) Mulk Raj Anand's eagerness to solicit for his novels—especially the Lalu Trilogy—the shadow of the *Mahabharata*, and, (b) Ngugi Wa Thiong'o's allusions to the *Book of Exodus* in the *Old Testament* in his works.

Anand has frequently remarked that the *Mahabharata* operates behind many of his works. Replying to a query in an interview regarding the use of the novel form for the depiction of colonial conditions, Anand says: "There is only one novel, that is, *Mahabharata*. In fact all my themes, situations and characters for novel writing are chosen from *Mahabharata*. That is a source book."[1] In another context, commenting on *Across the Black Waters*, he says that "*Across the Black Waters* may be a short book of the Mahabharatas being written all over the world by various writers all showing that in a war... few survive."[2] The majority of peasants in *The Village* who join the British Indian Army can understand the First World War only in terms of the *Mahabharata*:

> ... the war beyond the black waters was only another Mahabharata because the Angrezi Badsha was a cousin of the Badsha of Girmany (Germany), just as the Pandus were cousins of the Kurus. The principles of light and darkness, right and wrong, were arrayed on opposite sides, fighting for supremacy, and all the powerful kingdoms within reach were drawn into the

> struggle as in the old days of the great war of Kurukshetra (329).

One must remember that the Mahabharata could have been averted had Kauravas made an allowance of just five hamlets in a vast empire to the Pandavas, their cousins. It was the refusal to concede minimal land to the cousins that made war inevitable. Anand may not extensively employ the *Mahabharata* in his fiction (excluding the 'autobiographical' novels). In fact, he does not use myths from his own culture as widely as Ngugi does from his. The "mythic design is unfamiliar strategy to Anand," as Meenakshi Mukherjee points out (*Critical Essays on Indian Writing in English*, 200). Nevertheless one has to acknowledge that this epic at times shows itself as an important background. Part of the postscript to *Apology for Heroism* is from the *Mahabharata*. The way the black dog Kalu in *The Village* accompanies Lalu to the boundaries of the city when Lalu has to depart from Europe, is reminiscent of a similar scene in *Mahabharata*: a dog accompanying the eldest Pandava brother, Yudhishtira, to the end of the world. What is important is that it is with regard to the question of land that the Scriptures are employed.

Ngugi too enhances the significance of his works through repeated allusions to *The Exodus*. In *Weep Not, Child*, the Gikuyu people are compared to the children of Israel:

> "Gikuyu people, whose land had been taken by white men, were no other than the children of Israel... So although all men were brothers, the black people had a special mission to the world because they were the chosen people of God" (49).
>
> God would not let His people alone. The children of Israel must win (72).

Kihika, a Mau-Mau hero in *A Grain of Wheat* too visualizes the Gikuyu people as the children of Israel. As a boy he is deeply moved by the story of Moses and used to recount it to people. Kihika tells Mugo:

> ... not even miracles could make Pharaoh let the children of Israel go. But at midnight, the Lord smote all the

> first-born in the land of Egypt, from the first born of Pharaoh that sat on the throne unto the first-born of the captive that was in dungeon. And all the first born of the cattle. And the following day, he let them go. That is our aim (217).

That Pharaoh corresponds to the white man is too obvious to need elaboration. Allusions to *The Exodus*, the "Promised land" and prophets are frequent. For instance, the lines

> And the Lord spoke unto Moses
> Go unto Pharaoh, and say unto him,
> Thus faith the Lord
> Let my people go
> Exodus 8:1 (37).

Underlined in red in the hero Kihika's personal Bible, serve as an introduction to Chapter Four of—*A Grain of Wheat.* Kihika's sister Mumbi, who is a freedom fighter identifies herself with Esther of Old Testament: "In the Old Testament she often saw herself as Esther: So she revelled in that moment when Esther finally answers King Ahasuera's question and dramatically points at Haman, saying: "The adversary and enemy is the wicked Haman" (89).

A number of critics have contemplated on the profusion of biblical allusions in Ngugi's works. According to Emmanuel Ngara they heighten the "symbolic significance" of his works; "the language of the Bible and of religion in general becomes an object of analysis in its own right." Discussing the importance of the quotation from *The Exodus* that serves as an introduction to Chapter Four of *A Grain of Wheat,* Ngara says that it "refers to the liberation of the people of Kenya. The theme of deliverance of the children of Israel is transferred from its Bible context to the Kenyan situation, where there is a struggle for the liberation of the people of Kenya from British imperialism" (*Stylistic Criticism and the African Novel,* 89-90).[3] Eustace Palmer perceives Ngugi's use of the Bible thus: "a biblical aura is most appropriate for the descriptions of a people in bondage" (*Introduction to African Novel,* 9). One may take advantage of the observations of these critics and note that references, not only to the Bible, but to prophetic figures particularly, are insistent in Ngugi.

It is the urgency of the need for a prophet that often makes a character in Ngugi think that his is the prophetic role. Waiyaki in *The River Between* in a crucial moment of the novel's progression contemplates his own position as a saviour in the divided society:

> They called him a saviour. His own father had talked of a Messiah to come. Whom was the Messiah coming to save? From what? And where would He lead the people? Although Waiyaki did not stop to get clear answers to these questions, he increasingly saw himself as the one who would lead the tribe to light (101).

Njoroge in *Weep Not, Child*, imagines himself a Saviour while talking to Mwihaki about the dangers concerning the land and the people: "He remembered David rescuing a whole country from the curse of Goliath" (94); "he felt as he had felt when the old preacher talked about Sin. If Gikuyu people had sinned, then God might send him to them. He remembered Samuel and many other prophets" (94-95). Mugo in *A Grain of Wheat* thinks himself a saviour, a Moses, on many occasions. He has often heard the voice of God: "And God called out to him in a thin voice, Moses, Moses. And, Mugo cried out, Here am I, Lord" (143). Again he hears the voice the day before he confesses the guilt in front of the people, on the Uhuru (Independence) day: "And the voices faded into one voice from God calling out, Moses, Moses! And Mugo was ready with his answer: Here am I, Lord" (214). Kihika too, in *A Grain of Wheat*, tries to assume a prophetic role.

Scriptural figures are invoked by Ngugi to bring out the poignancy in the black's predicament in the colonial world. The Gikuyu people are shown anxiously awaiting the arrival of a prophet who will relate them to their land. The native consciousness preserves the memory of a time when a prophet had indeed appeared only to betrayed by the 'wicked.' Ngotho in *Weep Not, Child* narrates to the children the moment of the arrival of a Saviour:

> Once in the country of the ridges where the hills and ridges lie together like lions, a man rose. People thought that he was the man who had been sent to drive away the white man. But he was killed by wicked people because he said people should stand together (26).

The significance of history lies in the possibility of its re-enactment in the present. What happened in the past is about to repeat in the present. A prophet is expected to appear now, precisely because he had appeared in history. Njoroge, like many other natives in *Weep Not, Child,* believes Jomo Kenyatta to be the saviour of the black people:

> For Njoroge was sure that he had read about him in the Old Testament. Moses had led the children of Israel from Misri to the promise land. And because black people were really the children of Israel, Moses was no other than Jomo himself. It was obvious (50).

Boro, Njoroge's elder brother, calls Jomo the "Black Moses" (43). Kiarie, the spokesman at the strike organized in Njoroge's village, informs the gathering about Jomo: "There was a man sent from God whose name was Jomo. He was the Black Moses empowered by God to tell the White Pharaoh Let my people go!" (58).

The urgent need for the prophet prompts not only good characters like Waiyaki and Njoroge to imagine that they have been assigned prophetic roles but also makes room for false prophets and hence the frequent warning to guard against these latter ones. The topic of the sermon delivered by the priest in *Weep Not, Child* is 'land', and the sermon is accompanied by a reading from *St. Matthew* about false prophets:

> 'For many shall come in My name,
> saying, I am Christ, and shall
> deceive many'
> ... And many false Prophets shall
> rise, and shall deceive many (90).

It may be worth dwelling a little more on this extraordinary insistence on prophets, both genuine and fake, in Ngugi's work: The whole of Thabai village in *A Grain of Wheat*, for example, worships Mugo as the hero of the national freedom struggle. Many stories are woven around him:

> ... in detention Mugo had been shot at and no bullet would touch his skin. Through these powers, Mugo had been responsible for many escapes from detention of men who later went to fight in the forest. And who but Mugo could have smuggled letters from the camps to Members of Parliament in England? ... Mugo do miracles or even speak to God (143-4).

People are understandably shocked to learn that Mugo has betrayed a 'saviour' figure, Kihika. Mugo's confession on the Uhuru Day reveals the false Moses in him. The people of Thabai village had worshipped Mugo as a hero of the freedom struggle and wanted to honour him on Independence Day for the supposed sacrifice he made for the nation's liberation; it was also their design to dishonour and punish those who had sold themselves to the white man and betrayed the liberation movement. They had thought Karanja, a home guard and white man's black colleague, was the one who had betrayed Kihika, the hero of the Mau-Mau struggle. But Mugo's confession that he, a friend of Kihika, (and not Karanja) had acted as police informer, shocks them. The eponymous hero of *Matigari* is another prophet-figure. Matigari, "the patriot who survived the bullets," roams the land in demand of truth and justice. People are amazed at the stories of Matigari's miraculous escape, and come to believe that Matigari is Moses:

> 'This is truly amazing. And yet sceptics still don't believe in miracles! What more proof do they need?'
>
> 'You know, some people read about all the miracles done by Moses and they think that all those are just biblical myths.'
>
> 'Of course miracles happen...'
>
> 'Don't you know that the Bible says he shall come back again?' (81).

The talk of the arrival of the messiah is always in the air in Ngugi's fictional world. In *Matigari* the natives' expectancy of the prophet's arrival is so high as to greatly disturb the oppressive political establishment, which seeks the assistance of the Church to quell the belief. "Beware of the false prophets"—the priest warns, quoting *Matthew*:

> 'Then if any shall say unto you, lo, here is Christ, or there, believe it not. For there shall arise false Christs, and false Prophets, and shall show great signs and wonders in so much that if it were possible, they shall deceive the very elect. Behold, I have told you before' (105).

The recurrent topic of the prophet's arrival and the promised land argues the imperative to "place" the people in land.

Mulk Raj Anand and Ngugi Wa Thiong'o perceived that colonial conditions offered, as it were, laboratory conditions to study the manner in which man's spiritual needs seek political expression through the image of land. Frantz Fanon says:

> For a Colonized people, the most essential value, because the most concrete, is first and foremost the land: the land which will bring them bread and, above all dignity (*The Wretched of the Earth*, 34).

Hence, for the colonized, land symbolizes the past and all that is associated with the past—identity and dignity in particular; for the colonizer it is the supreme index of his power, might and dominance. This chapter examines—with special reference to *The Village* and *Weep Not, Child*—the clash of attitudes of the colonizer and the colonized towards land.

Set in the years preceding the First World War, *The Village*—Part I of 'Lalu' Trilogy—depicts the peasants' struggle to keep their few acres of land intact. The landlord Harbans Singh and the moneylender Seth Chaman Lal (who are the colonial government's making) are largely responsible for alienating the people from their rightful heritage. The entire village is in the process of losing land to the landlord and the moneylender. Nihal Singh who embodies in him all the noble qualities of a villager, struggles against these forces right up to his very last breath. Lalu, Nihal's youngest son inherits many of the qualities of his father—love of land, family and the village in particular but differs with him in his attitude towards technology. It is his 'modern' outlook that impresses the white sahib Mr. Hercules Long when he visits Lalu's village. Mr. Long's selection of Lalu for the leadership of the Boy Scout Movement in the village paves the way for Lalu's emergence as the "village hero." Too servile to object to the white man's choice, Harbans and his group envy Lalu. The antagonistic feelings they breed against Lalu and his people sharpen the conflict in the village. Because of his progressive views, Lalu is falsely charged with theft and he flees the village and joins the army in order to escape police arrest. Lalu's elder brother Sharm Singh is hanged to death for murdering the landlord's son Hardit (whom he catches red-handed) while having an affair with Kesari (Sharm Singh's wife). Another brother Dayal Singh whose marriage is foiled, turns into an ascetic. And the people lose all their land to Harbans, at the end. The novel closes with Lalu leaving for the war front in Europe across the seas and carrying with him the vision of his village.

Weep Not, Child is set during the National Liberation Movement of Kenya led by Mau-Mau. It presents the picture of a village community that disintegrates as a colonial settlement resulting in the alienation of people from their ancestral, God-given land. The situation is brilliantly fictionalized in the portrait of Ngotho who (like Nihal in *The Village*) is an embodiment of native culture. He works as a labourer and lives as an 'ahoi'[4] (squatter) on his ancestral lands now owned by the white settler Mr. Howlands and his native aid Jacobo. Land is the visible symbol for Ngotho of his ancestry and God, as well as the means of establishing contact with the ancestral spirits whose guidance is essential for his living. Although his sons—especially Boro the eldest—resent his 'inaction,' *i.e.*, his 'waiting' (instead of acting) for the white man to go, Ngotho does not regret the humiliation of being only a worker on his own land, because at least this provides an opportunity for him to keep in touch with his ancestral spirits, and with the past. Later, when Ngotho learns of Howland's claim that the land is the latter's 'home' (32), he realizes the inevitability of 'action' and doubts his wisdom in 'waiting' for the fulfilment of the ancient prophecy that the lands would be returned to hereditary owners with the exit of the white man. He participates in the strike that promises him the land. Ngotho understands that the strike would fail. That is the reason for his outrage against Jacobo, when the latter is brought to pacify the striking people. Ngotho's action against Jacobo, the black-white man, is backed by the people and he becomes the "hero of the hour" (59). The strike fails and, as expected, Ngotho's contact with his land is completely severed. He never approves of Boro's involvement with Mau-Mau; but, when Boro refuses to renounce Mau-Mau, Ngotho blesses him "to fight well". He dies, asking his youngest son Njoroge to look after the family. Njoroge who had pinned all his hope on education who had dreamt of living "a new and better home for the whole family" (1) ends up as a worker in the Indian shop. At the end, his suicide bid fails as his mother saves him.

Each of these novels, *The Village* and *Weep Not, Child,* is set in a small village, but the roads are suggestively laid by each writer across the seas to the war front in Europe. In *The Village*, the effort made by simple peasants to hold on to their land paradoxically forces them to join the army and they are sent away to fight the Germans in far away Europe. Their own land becomes the "promised land"—promised by the British Sarkar as reward for the sepoys who will distinguish themselves in the war. At the very beginning of each novel, the reader is sensitized to an important detail: the peasants' life in a colony is ultimately and inevitably environed by a battle-field beyond the border of his own village. Towards the end of *The Village*, Nihal's young son Lalu joins the army and leaves for Europe. But the unavoidable fate is indicated in the beginning. We see Nihal passing on to Lalu a heritage: the memory of a war that took place between the Sikhs and the English. The Sikhs are a warrior people for whom wearing a sword is as mandatory as wearing the turban. They are at once of a military and agricultural temperament. In either of these temperaments they are an exploited lot. Young Sikhs join the army to fight the colonizer's enemy. They are sucked into a destructive military activity, which wants in meaning. In *Weep Not, Child*, young men like Boro, Kori and Lieutenant have to take to arms for a cause without purpose, as seen in a conversation between Boro and his Lieutenant (of the Mau-Mau army): 'Why then do we fight?' asks Lieutenant. 'To kill,' replies Boro, 'Unless you kill, you'll be killed. So you go on killing and destroying. It's a law of nature. The White man too fights and kills with gas, bombs and everything'. 'But don't you think there's something wrong in fighting and killing unless you're doing so for a great cause like ours?' remarks Lieutenant. 'What great cause is ours?' enquires Boro. Lieutenant apprises Boro, 'why, Freedom and the return of our lost heritage.' 'May be something in it', says Boro, 'But for me Freedom is meaningless unless it can bring back a brother I lost. Because it can't do that, the only thing left to me is to fight, to kill and rejoice at any who falls under my sword' (102-3).

It is an irony that in both *The Village* and *Weep Not, Child* young people who have to till the land are compelled to take up arms. References to a big war appear early in *Weep Not, Child.* The road across the land leads one to the sea, and "across the seas was a big war" (5). The road running to the city is the road of mirages and delusions. On hot days, it shows little lakes that disappear and appear again at a distance. They are called "devil's waters":

> There was only one road that ran right across the land. It was long and broad and shone with black tar, and when you travelled along it on hot days you saw little lakes ahead of you. But when you went near, the lakes vanished, to appear again a little farther ahead. Some people called them the devil's waters because they deceived you and made you more thirsty if your throat was already dry (5).

In both Anand and Ngugi, one sees a striking similarity in attitude when roads are concerned. A road that may render people landless is resented. Lalu's thoughts regarding roads (in *The Sword and the Sickle*) run thus: "And this Sarkar had built roads and begun to push the peasants out of them by rolling up their land, the land which had belonged to them for generations, and donating it to whoever the Ferungis liked" (188). Nihal Singh's (in *The Village*) antipathy for the road constructed by order of George V. when he was crowned Emperor of Hindustan is understandable. It "had only meant a rise in the taxes of Nihal Singh" (20). Compare Nihal's and Lalu's thoughts relating to roads (quoted above) with the anxious thoughts of villagers in *Petals of Blood.* A group of Khaki clad engineers appear in the village of Ilmorog. As they walk through the fields, they are "besieged by the whole community who wanted to know what they were doing." When one of the engineers says that they are making "a preliminary survey for a proposed road across Africa," a villager "voicing the fear of the whole community" reacts: "I hope they will not take our lands away" (35).

This is not to say Ngugi and Anand are not clear-sighted about the great services that roads have rendered to mankind. A road for them could have negative associations when (a) it makes people homeless, (b) when it leads the natives only to destruction like a war and (c) when it seems laid only for an alien to arrive and settle in the natives land. It is "good to have a proper road" says Njuguna—a representative figure of the native culture—in *Petals of Blood.* "It will make our travel easy and we can send our goods to markets far away instead of giving it to these scorpions who visit us from the city" (35). Pondering over the proposed Trans African International Highway through Ilmorog, Munira, one of the protagonists, feels like laughing at the 'preposterous idea': "Why, I asked myself, had they not built smaller serviceable roads before thinking of international highways" (48). Cycling on the treacherous road that links Ilmorog to Ruwa-ini, capital of Chiri district, Munira remembers the 'past' of this road:

> The road had once been a railway like joining Ilmorog to Ruwa-ini. The line had carried wood and charcoal and wattle barks from Ilmorog forests to feed machines and men at Ruwa-ini. It had eaten the forests, and after accomplishing their task, the two rails were removed, and the ground became a road—a kind of road—that

> now gave no evidence of its former exploiting glory (11). There should be no difficulty in making out what Ngugi's notion of the road to "progress" is.

Not when it dislocates a people but when it relates them meaningfully to the world around, is a road approved by the two writers. Anand's short novel, *The Road*, well exemplifies this point. The theme here is the construction of the road that will link the remote village Govardhan to the city. Set in post-independence India, *The Road* offers a positive symbol of the road. The construction of the road would mean prosperity to the village. Further, the untouchables would become wage earners, thereby approaching the caste Hindus in human dignity. The caste Hindus resent the construction; they will not "touch the stones because they are felled by ... untouchables" (2). The landlord Thakur Singh owns the land on which the untouchables live, and the landlord's son Sanju, with his friend Lachman's help, burns down the huts of the untouchables. Lachman's father, Lambardar Dhooli Singh, though himself a Hindu, rehabilitates the untouchables in his own field, and takes up the construction of the road as a challenge. "The road will be built anyhow" (*The Road*, 7), he tells Thakur Singh, and as a result of this bold decision the engagement between the children of these two families is broken. Dhooli Singh's son later repents his rash act and joins the others in building the road. The landlord's son too repents for a while and works for the construction of the road. The road is finally built, with almost the whole village involving itself in the construction. At the end of the novel, the untouchable boy Bikhu walks towards Delhi "where no one knew who he was and where there would be no caste or outcaste" (111). In this novel, the road is not laid to make it accessible to an exploiting outsider. In the contrary, it is one that elevates the financial and human condition of village folk. And Anand presents it with approval. Viewed thus, *The Road* is not after all 'a timid work" as Saros Cowasjee puts it in *So Many Freedoms* (163). The road operates as a potent metaphor in the novel. On the penultimate page of the book the untouchable Bikhu is slapped by Sanju, the landlord's son, for accepting a tumbler of water from Rukmani. There is an attraction between Bikhu and the landlord's daughter, but in the great part of the novel neither of them can become adequately conscious of his/her feelings for the other. Bikhu is too conscious of his untouchability to face Rukmani. It is only when the road is completed that he can bring himself to look at Rukmani in the face. That Rukmani too can summon courage to offer a brass tumbler to an untouchable is the result of the road construction. Working for the road, the untouchables have earned wages; lost their huts but have discovered that the world is not confined to their village. Bikhu looks forward to better future in Delhi. The road to Delhi may not lead to an "effective solution" as Cowasjee says (*So Many Freedoms*, 163), but certainly has positive connotations. It should be granted at least than on completion of the road the untouchability Bikhu and Rukmani become human enough to look each other in the face.

Closely related to their attitudes to the road is the stand that Anand and Ngugi adopt with regard to towns. The town, which is the alien colonizer's making, is spoken of with subtle disrespect and resentment. In *The Village* some of the fraudulent traits of the town are those that link it to the English colonizer—going by some of the figures that Lalu notices when at the fair. For example, there is, on the Grand Trunk Road, a city quack who sells the "Elixir of life" to gullible peasants. It is a medicine that will make the "impotent potent in a day" (108) boasts the seller, like an "unashamed brazen actor." The appeal is based on the claim that the ancient wisdom of the Himalayan sages which has gone into the preparation of the 'Elixir' is proved by the "numerous letters sent (to the quack) by the kings of Europe, asking for the medicine" (107). "The feeble" are made "strong like the lions," claims the seller. The Havildar in the fair, who is trying to lure the gullible peasants into the English army, makes the same false appeal to the lion-like character of the peasants. The Havildar, acting for the English rulers shows the same falsity as the quack. He addresses the young villagers as 'traditional warriors,' 'Sikhs sprung from the loins of tigresses,' and asks them to join the English army, for, the English are the "friends of the poor," "these angrez log, truly they are born fighters... lions like us..." (110). There is the lure of money too in the appeal.

The big-mouthed peddlers promote their goods and ideas by advertising that they are in demand among the whites. And what is good for the whites must be better for the natives. A prominent feature of the Kipanga town in *Weep Not, Child* is the business establishments of the Indian traders whose first customers are not natives, but the white settlers:

> The Indian shops were many. The Indian traders were said to be rich. They too employed some black boys whom they treated as nothing... White settlers with their wives and children often came to the rich Indians and bought all they wanted (7).

The atmosphere of the town is congenial to the promotion of crime: "Some young men spent all their time doing nothing but loitering in the shops... They were called the lazy boys and the people in the village said that such men would later turn to stealing and crime" (8). The town Kipanga is spoken of as a favourite haunt of young men who murder and rob.

The town in *The Village* is similarly rendered. Early in the novel we find old Nihal Singh muttering to himself. 'It is strange how every time I go to town I feel nearer death' (4). A little later he tells Lalu: '... I have never liked the town of Manabad which... the Ferungis (whites) have built' (4). It may appear rather old for writers like Anand and Ngugi who had subscribed to the philosophy of progress to allow room for strong anti-city views in their works. But it should be mentioned here that the town or the city appears to earn the displeasure of these writers, only when it is imposed as part of colonizer culture, and not when it has ancient anchorage in native culture. The description of Daulatpur in *Coolie* should support this observation. This is a city with its own cultural past, a city that symbolizes the history, traditions and customs of the land. It is with a sense of pride that Anand captures the glory of Daulatpur through the consciousness of Munoo, who as a school boy has read about it. It is one of "the two oldest and most important (cities) in Northern India... said to have been founded by Maharaja Daulat Singh, the Rajput King." Daulatpur is indirectly associated with the mythological figure Rama. It had been the scene of various battles in history, having been conquered by Mahmud Ghaznawi, the idol-breaker and looter of the buried treasures of the temple of Somnath. He wondered whether Mahmud had plundered any gold or jewels from the temple he had just visited. But he remembered that Akbar, the great Moghal, had given money to the priests of the city and encouraged their religion. The Sikhs had defeated the Moghals outside the town and Ranjit Singh had given away its old houses to his beloved councillors. But the Angrezi (English) Sarkar had conquered it before the mutiny.

The resplendent figures of all the kings of India, as they appeared in the pictures of his history book, passed before his eyes, garlanded with rows upon rows of necklaces, with plumes in their turbans and jewels on their dresses. 'This city was,' he thought, 'when my village did not exist' (73).

Daulatpur is one place where an Indian employs Munoo. In Sham Nagar, he was a servant to 'black European' Nathoo Ram; in Bombay he worked in the white ruler's factory and in Simla he is employed by a white woman. Munoo is relatively happy here in Daulatpur. He is as poor as he was in Sham Nagar but he is "at home". Munoo keeps comparing Sham Nagar and Daulatpur and the comparison is in favour of Daulatpur. Any town or spot that suggest its own past, and is not a creation of the colonizer's commands Munoo's (and the readers') admiration. The rendering of the hill town Kalka for instance, confirm this:

> The sight of stray houses on the slopes of the mountains took him back to his own home, and he had the feeling that it was only yesterday that he had left the village in the valley. A ruined fortress, which capped a far distant peak encouraged the illusion because it looked like the crumbling temple of Durga near Hamirpur, and the angry nullahs that gorged their way through the fastnesses

> of these mountains completed the vague similarity... He was beginning to feel in his proper element (*Coolie*, 256).

But the town, when considered as colonizer's making, is a desecrated part of the sacred land. Lalu and Nihal are alert to the difference between the sacred and not-so-sacred parts of the land. The same sense of the sacred is evident in Ngotho and Njoroge in *Weep Not, Child.* Consider Ngotho's feelings:

> The school looked a strange place. But fascinating. The Church, huge and hollow, attracted him. It looked haunted. He knew it was the House of God. But some boys shouted while they were in there. This too shocked him. *He had been brought to respect all holy places like graveyards and the bush around the fig tree* (14) (Emphasis Added).

In *The Village* walking towards the village, Nihal Singh senses

> ... a kinship with the familiar earth. He felt the invisible warmth of the sheltered lives in the village where he was respected. He sniffed the air as if it were *nectar* and gazed upon the landscape as if it were *heaven* full of the ineffable *bliss of life*, full of *men* and *women* and *children* and *animals* and *fruits* and *flowers.* Only the deep red pits of cinder and the mounds of burnt clay near the brick factory blighted the view. But now he accepted that desecrated part of the fields also as the counterpart of the ploughed land as a netherworld, because it has been established years ago, and had become part of the landscape of the village (23) (Emphasis added).

Land is sacred because of its association with fertility; it is paradise on earth. Comparable are the feelings of Ngotho in *Weep Not, Child*:

> Ngotho left early for work... Ngotho loved the rainy seasons when everything was green and the crops in flower, and the morning dew hung on leaves. But the track where he had disturbed the plants and made the water run off made him feel if, through his own fault,

> he had lost something. There was one time where he had felt a desire to touch the dew-drops or open one and see what it held inside. He had trembled like a child but, after he had touched the drops and they had quickly lost shape melting into whiteness, he felt ashamed and moved on. At times he was thankful to Murungu for no apparent reason as he went through the cultivated fields all alone the whole country had a stillness (28).

It is because of such strong feelings for land and place that the most fertile part of the land is selected by Ngugi as the arena for the working out of the conflict between the black native and the white settler in *Weep Not, Child.* The ancestral part of the land of which Ngotho is too much a part "to be separated" (30) is the best place for the enactment of the conflict—"the best land in all the country" (32) as Ngotho says.

In the works of Anand and Ngugi, the sanctity of the land gets symbolically centred around an important geographical landmark: in Anand, the banyan or the pipal; in Ngugi, the mugumo. Interestingly, the banyan, the pipal and the mugumo are fig trees. Soon after the initiation, Waiyaki in *The River Between* is taken to the mugomo tree. He experiences excitement and fear. Standing on the hill top and beneath the tree he beholds the vision of a united country—because, from that vantage point, 'the warring ridges' appear to merge "into one area of beautiful land" (16). The mugumo tree is described thus:

> A big mugumo tree stood near the edge of the hill. It was a huge tree, thick and *mysterious.* Bush grew and bowed *reverently* around it. And there the *ancient* tree stood, *towering over the hill, watching as it were, the whole country. It looked holy and awesome, dominating Waiyaki's soul* so that he felt very small and in the *presence of a mighty* power. This was a *sacred tree.* It was the tree of Murungu (15). (Emphasis added)

Ngotho in *Weep Not, Child* describes the mugumo tree to the children thus:

> At the foot of Kerinyaga, a tree rose. At first it was a small tree and grew up, finding a way even through the darkness. It wanted to reach the light and the Sun. This tree had life. It went up, up, sending forth the rich warmth of a blossoming tree—you know a holy tree in the dark night of thunder and moaning. This was Mukuyu, God's tree. Now, you know that at the beginning of things there was only one man (Gikuyu) and one woman (Mumbi). It was under this Mukuyu that he first put them (23-24).

Matigari's journey in quest of land and freedom begins and ends at the mugumo tree, which is described reverentially:

> ... a huge *mugumo*, a fig tree, right in the middle of a cluster of other trees. It was remarkable for its very wide trunk, and its four roots were visible, with one jutting out from the middle, and three others sticking out at the sides (3-4).

In quite a few of Ngugi's short stories too the mugumo tree appears as major signifier of Gikuyu land and culture.

The parallel spot in Anand's world in the banyan tree (or the pipal, a fig tree of the same family as the banyan), sacred to the Hindus. The banyan may not serve a thoroughly religious purpose in Anand's works, but, it most certainly impresses us as the centre of the village. The image of the banyan has great potential to signify the uniqueness of Indian culture. The only place where Lalu could rest in the fair is under a banyan tree on the outskirts of the city:

> As he stretched himself to a restful position by the roots of a banyan tree, the fatigue of the night and the warmth, which the feeding of the 'inner gods' had produced, overpowered him even against his will, and he dozed off (The Village, 115).

There are numerous references to the banyan/pipal tree in *Untouchable* and other works of Anand. It is located often at close proximity to the place of worship, as the following examples show: (a) In *The Village*, the "square of the shrine is only partially obscured by the banyan." (b) In the *Untouchable*, "at the foot of the banyan tree is a miniature temple" (49). It is when he stands "in the shadow of the banyan tree that Bakha becomes inquisitive of the Hindu religion" (49). Repeated humiliations drive Bakha to seek shelter under the pipal tree: "He crept out of the ditch and made for a pipal tree, which stood in the plain surrounded by a clay platform. He sat down under it, facing the Sun" (*Untouchable*, 101). It is at the foot of the banyan tree that Bakha's nerves are "steadied." In the words of a perceptive critic,

> Anand rejects much in the Indian tradition. But he appreciates the supreme importance of Buddha's compassion. Therefore, one is empted, even at the risk of over-reading to associate Bakha's pipal tree with the tree of enlightenment. (Damodar Rao, "Afterword" to *Untouchable*, 142).

But Damodar Rao's insightful comment is limited to the analysis of *Untouchable*. The imposing banyan and the pipal tree are to be taken into account in the other works of Anand too. We are told in *The Village* for example, that for a "devout Sikh" tobacco smell is "anathema", and that in order to avoid the smell of tobacco cultivated by non-Sikhs, as well as the bazaar, Nihal Singh rushes "by the porch under the bearded banyan tree, which was the village centre" (25). Again in the short story, "The Tractor and the Corn Goddess," Anand dramatizes the conflict between tradition and modernity mostly beneath the banyan tree: "The crisis actually happened under the banyan tree" (130). A new landlord with progressive ideas introduces a tractor to lessen the peasant's burdensome work, but the villagers see it as a "monstrosity" that will "desecrate" the earth. The oldest villager says that the whites invent technical goods because they do not possess "Shiva Shakti" (God's energy), which is there in the "sinews" of the natives. But the kindly young landlord successfully explains that the new instrument can give the peasants enough time to enjoy their "rest under the shade of the banyan tree." The peasant who is made driver of the tractor expresses his acceptance: "I don't mind... if all of us can have really a fine siesta... In the hot weather there is no place like the shade of this banyan" (135). In *Coolie*, before leaving for town, Munoo is seen under the banyan tree. The banyan shelter has been for him the place of freedom and happiness. Before leaving the village, he shares stolen fruits with his friends beneath this tree:

> ... it was pleasant to sit here with his fellows, all little boys of the same age as himself, for when they had stolen enough fruit during their wanderings behind the cattle in the morning, they ate it in the humid, sweet-scented shade of the banyan tree (3).

These examples of the banyan and the mugumo in Anand and Ngugi mark the manner in which the land is sanctified by uniqueness. For the colonist one land is perhaps not different from another, except in terms of the material produce each may yield, but for a people who value freedom there exists a sense of uniqueness of their own land. The cultural importance of land in Anand and Ngugi is brought out by the prominence accorded to a fig tree in their works.

The conflicts between aliens and those who belong to the land are presented in terms of their attitudes to land. The aliens and their local agents comprehend land only in terms of money. In *The Village*, those who act as agents of the Sarkar grow cash crops like tobacco, mustard and vegetables. But true sons of the soil like Nihal and Harnam grow grain. It is on grain that tax is regularly hiked, says Harnam:

> They say they have raised the tax on grain. And I am told that the Sarkar is buying up the harvest cheap, and storing it in its granaries so that it can sell at a profit... How can they expect us to pay the taxes? (35).

Anand exposes the immorality of the colonial government that targets essential food grains for tax-hike, buying it cheaply from peasants and making huge profits by selling them at high prices. The village situation in *Weep Not, Child* is much the same. Pyrethrum, a cash crop, cannot be grown by all Africans. Only Jacobo, the rich landlord and chief of the Home guards is licensed to grow pyrethrum. The colonizer has established a system in which a few natives, like Jacobo and Harbans are used—and it is not individual whites using these people, but the system—to deprive the natives of the land. This explains why such 'agents' of the system become more hateful than the whites themselves, for they act not for themselves but for the whites, and convert the sacred land into a money-yielding commodity. It is in this sense that they are traitors to the land. Harbans Singh and Fazlu in *The Village* are treated with contempt because they see land not as one that fulfils human needs by giving grain, but as wares that can yield more and more cash.

An important feature of the colonial system as visualized by Anand and Ngugi is the 'profane' attempt to transform land into cash. This is why the cash-crop growers in their fictional worlds, even when they are natives, are viewed with disrespect: "Blackness is not all that makes a man" we are told in *Weep Not, Child*: "A white man is a white man. But a black man trying to be a white man is bad and harsh" (21). This is why Ngotho (in *Weep Not, Child*) is suddenly enraged when the native Jacobo intervenes to dissuade his own people from the strike. The strike-call (with the figure of Kenyatta at the back) was for a non-violent demonstration, but the appearance of Jacobo on behalf of the whites to pacify the agitators infuriates Ngotho:

> For one single moment Jacobo crystallized into a concrete betrayal of people. He became the physical personification of the long years of waiting and suffering—Jacobo was a traitor. Ngotho rose. He made his way towards the platform while everyone watched, wondering what was happening. He was now near Jacobo. The battle was now between these—Jacobo on the side of the white people and he on the side of the black people (58-9).

Ngotho's passion at that moment epitomizes the black's temper. Ngotho has been always looked up to by the blacks as a model. "His home was well-known for being a place of peace" (11). The "feeling of oneness" (40) in Ngotho's household is attributed to his stature. At the moment of Jacob's intervention during the strike, Ngotho naturally becomes the "hero of the hour" (60); and the people are morally behind his action against the black-white man Jacobo.

A character in *The Village* that corresponds to Jacobo in *Weep Not, Child* is Harbans Singh, the landlord of Nandpur. Harbans is a native feigning to be white. Summing up Fanon's argument in his Foreword to *Black Skin White Masks,* Homi Baba remarks: "the colonized can only imitate, never identify" (XXI). Fanon's book is a study in the psychic condition of the colonized who desperately yearn to imitate the white. The white-masked black men assume that their destiny lies in becoming white ("turn white or disappear"). Fanon writes of the black man's notion of white skin:

> The black man wants to be white... black men want to prove to white men at all costs, the richness of their thoughts, the equal value of their intellect (*Black Skin, White Masks,* 228).

Harbans Singh's odious mimicking of the whites is imagistically worked out by Anand. Harbans is introduced to us as "leprous faced" (20); attention is drawn to his 'leprous-whiteness' (103). A more graphic description of the man is this one:

> ...a white bearded, stout, little man, cursed by God with leukadorma—a *disease that made his face the colour of an Englishman* in the tropics, and *endorsed it with disfiguring patches of brown* into the bargain (102) (Emphasis added).

It is certainly not Anand's intention to make fun of Harbans for the colour of his skin which he cannot help. But what Anand wants to convey is that Harbans is abnormal in his alignment with the white rulers. Harbans' physical abnormality is a symptom of his spiritual aberration. The diseased condition is accentuated by his aping of the English in dress and manners. At the time of the English collector Hercules Long's visit to the village, Harbans Singh dresses himself up like an Englishman, "severely buttoned in a black coat" over which there is "a loose-gold-brocaded coat with a Kaisar-i-Hind gold medal and various other insignia and decorations, his dumbbell legs compressed into light white fannel trousers" (186).

Ironically, the Englishman himself is very informally dressed "in the Khaki shirt, shorts and solar hat which he always wore, to which he had added a Kashmir tweed Norfolk jacket for warmth." While Mr. Long speaks in Hindi, Harbans Singh's speech is laboriously in English.

Todar Mal (in *Coolie*), a vakil and nominated member of the Municipal Committee of Daulatpur also belongs to Anand's 'black-white' category of men. Like Harbans Singh in *The Village.* Todar Mal also yearns for recognition, not by his own people but by the white man. A motive force behind his notable services to the colonizer was to solicit the white man's acknowledgement. His contributions to the colonial rule included among other things, a donation of twenty thousand rupees to His Excellency the Viceroy's war fund. He is adequately rewarded by the colonizer for his allegiance to the government and his active support: he is made public prosecutor in the Daulatpur courts, bestowed with a 'Knighthood' and is titled, 'Rai Bahadur.' The rulers treat him as a friend, natives regard him as a "traitor." for he had, during the political riots, taken refuge in the fort (82). It is because of his servility that Todar acts like a white man. His servile nature is seen in his costume, which is a mixture of the black-white colours. Todar is dressed in "a black alpaca frock coat, tight white cotton pyjamas and a great big heap of turban on his long black face" (80). The most resentful thing about him in his desperate desire to ape the behaviour of the white man. Todar's craze for the white man's identity matches well Fanon's observation, "turn white or disappear" (228). Todar Mal's disgusting servility is reminiscent of Gulliver's behaviour in the Honyhuhnm land. He is thrilled at the prospect of showing himself as the white man's companion. This is when the English Commissioner Dr. Marjoribanks has to go inspect the Cat Killers' Lane. Todar thinks he can take the Englishman in his gig and thus show himself off before the natives. But the white man "did not want to go riding in Sir Todar Mal's gig, as he had hated to be stared at and salaamed by all the 'niggers'" (86). The letter he writes to the English Commissioner, is studded with expressions betraying his servility:

> Honoured Sir,
>
> The omission on my part to *render you a tribute of the heart's* best *render* and *esteem* due from man to man in the shape of *occasional epistles* is, I have always felt, a wrong and such as I can *hardly plead any cause* to mitigate the enormity of. *I am* therefore *greatly ashamed to present myself* before you through the medium of this communication. Nevertheless, let me carry to you my cordial assurance that your name is *indelibly impressed* on the *tablet of my memory* as my greatest friend both inside and outside the Municipal Committee.
>
> Now *I have to request the honour of your visit* to Cat Killers' Lane, which is full of smoke on account of the burning of stone coal in the pickle factory next door to my house. *I shall be greatly honoured* if you do so...
>
> My services to the government are well known to you. I gave twenty thousand rupees to His Excellency the Viceroy's war fund, in recognition of which I have received the *splendid title of knighthood.* I hope that bearing in mind the services I have rendered to the *benign* Empire, you will come to rid me of the affliction of this smoke, which is a constant cause of worry, remorse and sorrow to me and mine.
>
> With my *wife's modest salaams* to Mrs. Majoribanks, *I am your most faithful servant* and ever *grateful memorialist* (84) (Emphasis added).

To the local eye, natives like Harbans, Todar Mal and Jacobo who ape the rulers in their lifestyle are more offensive than the whites, for they (*i.e.*, the black-whites) regard land not as a nourisher of body or spirit, but as a patch that can be unendingly squeezed for cash. A scene that illustrates this well is the one in which old Nihal approaches Seth Chaman Lal for a loan. The pledge offered by him is the corn he has grown on his land. The moneylender need not sell the crop, he pleads, for he "always hated to see his good corn, the corn he had sowed and reaped with love, sold for petty cash." "That crop is dear to me," he petitions (163). The moneylender, however can see no value in the grain. He dismisses the fruit of Nihal's labour with a diabolical grin, replying, "if I tramp in a sugarcane field, I might meet a snake. I am afraid" (163). For the true sons of the soil, money is not the measure of land. Nihal is vain tries to enlighten the moneylender of the peasants' value system: "We peasants don't count in terms of money... We have to count in terms of buffaloes, bullocks, cows, land and harvests" (164). A deeply disturbing shift in the notion of production is worked out throughout *The Village*. It is not vegetable and cash crops, but foodgrains that his heavily taxed. And, foodgrain is for village consumption, whereas a commercial crop is produced for a market beyond the village borders. The market as an inhuman abstraction is a threatening presence for the peasant in *The Village*. In the opening pages of the novel Nihal sees the landlord's bullock cart heading for the market, to sell cattle fodder; Fazlu is always excitedly talking of the prices his vegetables and onions are likely to fetch in the market. The simple peasants, on the other hand, know not the ways of the market. "How are we peasant folk to know the market conditions before hand"? Harnam asks. Further,

> How can we plan the crops so as not to produce too much or too little? But the Sarkar... will merely send the patwari to collect rent and takes the money on the yield without bothering about what prices the grain has fetched. Yet when I complained to tehsildar about it, he said, 'Bad condition will give you a better sense of the value of money' (297).

The tehsildar's remark is significant. It means that the common peasant is being forced to consider land in terms of only cash. When Nihal approaches the moneylender for a loan, the request for loan is prefaced by Sharm Singh, Nihal's son, thus: "There has been a lack of money this season" (160). Deficiency in money is chronic in the case of a peasant who grows only foodgrain. The effects of the increasing importance of cash crops are terrible for him. The commercialization of agriculture has resulted in the ever increasing demand for cash crops; but there is an inherent inability in the simple peasant to plan the production of foodgrain: "How can we plan the crops so as not to produce too much or too little?" Harnam Singh's question is crucial. Too little food results in a famine and in the failure to meet the farmer's need for money. On the other hand, too much production will certainly bring down the prices of grains, if urbanization does not keep pace with the increased yield. And this will only ensure further commercialization of crop! Subtly Anand depicts how land is turned into a market commodity. Harnam, Lalu's uncle relates to Lalu how the entire village has become landless because of the market conditions. "No prices at all, son?" ...merchants in the town say that the Sarkar is responsible, informs Harnam. It is because of such conditions created by the market economy that the whole village has to lose land to the landlord and the moneylender: "I have had to mortgage the whole of my land to Chaman Lal. But I am not the only one, almost the whole village is ruined" (290).

An important factor that sanctifies land is the past—used either as history or myth. Perhaps this is why in both *The Village* and *Weep Not, Child* fathers play important roles as transmitters of the cultural past to their sons. In both the novels there are times when the father's stature and relevance is questioned seriously. Ngotho's eldest son Boro is unsympathetic to his father's 'waiting' for the white man's voluntary exit and in his "superstitious belief" in the ancient prophecy. His angry whisper sounds like a shout: "To hell with the prophecy?" He questions his father: "How can you continue working for a man who has taken your land?" (27). On another occasion when Ngotho spoils the strike by his impulsive action, Boro treats him with contempt:

> Boro quarrelled much with the old man. He accused him of having spoilt everything by his rash action in spite of Kiarie's warning. Boro clearly had contempt for Ngotho... Ngotho as a result, had diminished in stature, often assuming a defensive secondary place whenever talking with his sons and their friends (71).

In *The Village* too, the father appears to suffer loss of stature. Lalu is displeased by the father's reverential attitude to the Mahant, who is a fraud; he has only contempt for Nihal's nostalgic recollection of the past. Lalu feels his father is cheated by city people, everywhere: "They all take advantage of you... because you are an old man" he comments (12-13). Lalu even teases his father for his frequent glorification of the past.

But in each of the novels the father's stature is reaffirmed at the end; and it is in the masterly manner in which the fathers give up life that the reaffirmation is made. When Lalu is abruptly called to the European war front, and a greatly disturbed Gujri (Lalu's mother) asks him to seek extension of leave, Nihal admonishes her for waiting in anticipation of his own demise and Lalu's departure:

> ... cease to mourn, weak woman. Cease to mourn for me and for him. Parents breed children not for themselves but to fight public causes. Let him go out to life and be a lion's son. Let him go out and perform deeds worthy of his fore-fathers. Let him go out and reap the harvest of experience (309).

Addressing the son who seeks his blessings at the time of parting, he instructs: "Be brave, son. Take courage, and don't be a jackal. Go and work with your hands and be happy, for you are young. And leave me to die if I have to die" (310). These are the words of a father who is on his death bed—his very last words in the novel.

Ngotho's conduct and utterance in the face of death in *Weep Not, Child* resemble Nihal's. He instructs his son Boro, whom he has failed to dissuade from Mau-Mau involvement, "All right. Fight well. Turn your eyes to Murungu and Ruriri (Gikuyu Gods). Peace to you all" (124). These are his last utterances.

In both novels, fathers see their sons, not as isolated creatures in the present period, but as responsible beings vitally connected to a past that houses historical and mythical ancestors. The peoples' struggle for the 'ancestral lands' in *The Village*, and *Weep Not, Child* becomes more meaningful in the light of his vital link between the past and the present. In *The*

Village, Nihal's narration of the Sikhs' battles against the English informs Lalu that not only Nihal, but many of Lalu's ancestors had participated in these battles. Nihal relates to Lalu the war in which he fought the British, when he was young:

> The Khalsa had drunk nectar from the foot of the Durbar Sahib and vowed to be united as one man after the death of Maharaja Ranjit Singh. If it hadn't been for those vile ministers who turned traitors, the Punjab would never have been conquered by the ferungis (14).

Ironically, a man like Nihal had fought for the homeland is deprived of his hereditary lands, while Harbans's father who had betrayed the native land is given that land and made the landlord of the village.

Ngugi delineates the importance of land to Gikuyu people in terms of the legends concerning the land. In *The River Between*, Waiyaki gets to know the legend of the land from his father Chege on the day of his (Waiyaki's) second birth ceremony:

> .... It was before Agu; in the beginning of things. Murungu brought the man and woman here and again showed them the whole vastness of the land. He gave the country to them and their children and the children of the children, tene na tene, world without end (18).

This legend recurs in *Weep Not, Child.* Story-telling is an important activity in Ngotho's household and Ngotho's story to his children is about the first man and first woman that God created and about the blessing they received from Him:

> This land I hand over to you. O Man and Woman
> It's your to rule and till in serenity sacrificing
> Only to me, you're God, under my sacred tree (24).

This consciousness of their own past makes the question of land a piercing one. "Where did the land go?" asks Ngotho (and later Njoroge) "Where O creator went our promised land?" (25).

Eustace Palmer in his analysis of *Weep Not, Child* records the importance of the Gikuyu and Mumbi myth, the spiritual significance of land to Ngotho, and the commercial interest that land chiefly holds for the white settler Howlands (*Introduction, 1-2*). Palmer finds it interesting to compare Ngotho's attitude to land with that of Howlands. According to Palmer, "Howlands loves the land in his own way, with the satisfaction of possession and subjugation; Ngotho on the other hand, reveres his land" (2). Continuing the comparison, Palmer writes:

> (Howlands') own claims to the land albeit the claims of the conqueror, are set beside those of Ngotho and fairly balanced. Ngugi also demonstrates the equal admiration both men have for the land, and his tone of voice in the relevant passages suggests that he does not despite Howlands. Moreover, the histories and fortunes of the two men are strikingly similar. Both of them experienced the First World War and ended up disillusioned with Britain. Both feel alienated from Britain (Mr. Howlands now regards Kenya as his home and, if anything, hates Britain more than Ngotho). Both lost promising sons in the Second World War. Both are plagued with doubt as to whether their sons—Stephen and Njoroge—on whom responsibility would now devolve, are adequate for the task. It is obvious that... Ngugi is doing his best to elicit the reader's sympathy for Mr. Howlands. As Mr. Howlands and Ngotho survey the *shamba* together, we see them as two men with similar histories and doubts (8).

It is necessary to quote the long passage from Palmer to examine a little more the manner in which Howlands and Ngotho stake their claims. It is true that Howlands speaks of the land as his 'god' but the crucial difference between Ngotho's and Howlands' attitude to land is that the farmer is ever eager to affirm his past in relation to the land, whereas Howlands is equally anxious to erase his past. Howlands has "escaped" the war. But the past catches up with him, and he has to act for the whites in England, when he is appointed District Officer:

> "He now knew may be there was no *escape*. The present that had made him a D.O. reflected a past from which

> he had tried to *run away*. The *past had followed him* even though he had tried to *avoid politics*, government, and anything else that might *remind him of that betrayal* (76) (Emphasis added).

Howlands's past contains an act of betrayal that he would like to forget totally. The escapist attitude is much in evidence in expressions like "escape," "to run away" "past had followed," "avoid politics" and "remind him of that betrayal." A contradiction exists in Howlands that must invalidate his moral claims over the land: "To submit to his wife was to listen to the voice of England. No. He would not give in either to Mau-Mau or his wife" (77). There is too, a disunity in the Howlands household. Howlands categorically denies that his home is England—for that is where his unsavoury past lies. On the other hand, his wife, frustrated because she could have no sensational experience in life, and harassed by sheer ennui, would like to affirm that her home in England. It is significant that behind his contradiction, behind his affirmation and denial, there are only negative dispositions. If Howlands is angry with the Mau-Mau, it is because they remind him of his past, which he would like to reject:

> And who were these Mau-Mau who were claiming that land, his god? Ha, ha! He would have laughed at the whole ludicrous idea, but for the fact that they had forced him into the other life, the life he had tried to avoid. He had been called upon to take up a temporary appointment as a District Officer. He had agreed. But only because this meant defending his god. If Mau-Mau claimed the only thing he believed in, they would see! Did they want to drive him back to England, the forgotten land? They were mistaken (77).

Palmer says that Ngotho, like Howlands, feels 'alienated from Britain.' That would be without meaning, for Britain *is* an alien land for the Kenyan. The crucial difference between Howlands and Ngotho is that for the farmer there is a land to be "forgotten" and for the other there exists a "promised land." This may greatly explain why the "only thing left to him (Howlands) was hatred" (127-8). Because of the conflict between what is to be "forgotten" and what is "promised", crisis reaches a peak. As Kamau, Njorge's brother puts it, "I tell you there's no safety anywhere. There's no hiding in this naked land" (83).

The conflict between the natives and the whites in *The Village* is not a direct as in *Weep Not, Child.* The white sahib Mr. Hercules Long in *The Village* is not a settler, like Howlands. But there is a certain negative quality in the District Commissioner Mr. Long's past. His past contains no rightful 'placement' of the man in his own homeland and amidst his own people. His birth was in India, but he was brought up mostly in England. He has arrived in India only recently. His early schooling had been at Bishop Cotton School in Simla, where he constantly complained of ragging by other English boys. When this sulky boy was exhorted to live up to his name 'Hercules,' he asserted himself by thrashing not the English boys who ragged him, but an Indian boy! And Hercules's earlier Christian names were Henry and Havelock, both of which were the names of his maternal grandfathers who had fought in the Indian Mutiny. That is to say, his past consists of memories relating not to his own homeland, but somebody else's. This is a condition similar to Howlands's! Both share the same uncertainty in 'belonging'. We are told Mr. Long is unlike the other Englishmen, not of course in his attitude to the Indians and their land; but only in the mode he adopts to keep the natives subjugated. He is abnormally eager to exhibit that he wants to be familiar with simple peasants but Anand shows that this condescending man is a misfit in the Indian village. In a comic episode Mr. Hercules Long is scared to death by a harmless buffalo and ridiculously climbs a tree in an effort to save himself. Surely, a man who wants to link his life with peasants cannot wish the cattle away! There is the subtlety with which Anand demolishes any authenticity in the claims to land by the whites—especially the 'kindly,' 'progressive' ones.

NOTES

1. See Appendix B, "Conversations with Mulk Raj Anand," p. 145.

2. In a letter dated 8 October, 1995. See Appendix C, p. 151.

3. Clifford B. Robson in his analysis of *The River Between* focuses on the use of Christian myth. He points out that the original title of *The River Between* was *The Black Messiah.* This may indicate the extent to which Ngugi sees the importance of biblical images for reflecting African situation under colonialism. The use of biblical symbols and images is quite appropriate as the novel partly "deals with the mission at work." Also, as Robson points out, "In *The River Between* the idea of saviour follows closely, in some respects, the story of Christ—a chosen man, doing his father's will, ignored by most of his fellow men and sacrificed for the sake of others" (Ngugi Wa Thiong'o, 16).

   David Cook and Okenimpke comment on Ngugi's adherence to Christian symbolism thus: "Christianity is admired and accepted, and yet is also looked at critically and askance, till eventually it loses authority. Since Njoroge formulates his Christian beliefs in parrot fashion, the reader remains skeptical of their validity" (*Ngugi wa Thiong'o: An Exploration of His Writings,* 62).

   It is significant to note that in 1970 Ngugi cast aside, as part of his anti-colonial stand, his Christian name and his Christianity. Killam observes the impact of the Church on the Kenyan life thus: "The Church in Kenya, as it was over all of Africa during the imperial period, was in the vanguard in bringing about irreversible historical change. Ngugi traces this influence against the background of some seventy-five years of Kenyan history in his novels" (*An Introduction to the Writings of Ngugi,* 9).

4. 'Ahoi' is a Gikuyu system of land tenure. Jomo Kenyatta explains: "'Muhoi' (ahoi) is one who acquires cultivation rights of the lands of another man or family unit, on a friendly basis without any payment for the use of land." See *Facing Mount Kenya,* 22. Ngugi's father himself was an ahoi on the land of an African landlord. See *Detained: A Writer's Prison Diary.*

WORKS CITED

Anand, Mulk Raj. *Across the Black Waters.* 1940. Bombay: Kutub-Popular, 1955.

Anand, Mulk Raj. *Apology for Heroism.* 1946. Bombay: Kutub-Popular, 1980.

Anand, Mulk Raj. *Coolie.* 1936. New Delhi: Penguin, 1993.

Anand, Mulk Raj. *The Road.* 1961. New Delhi: Sterling Publishers, 1987.

Anand, Mulk Raj. *The Tractor and the Corn Goddess and Other Stories.* Bombay: Thacker and Company, 1947. New Delhi: Arnold Publishers, 1987.

Anand, Mulk Raj. *The Village.* London: Jonathan Cape, 1939.

Anand, Mulk Raj. *Untouchable.* 1935. Mysore: Geetha Book House, 1995.

Baba, Homi. Foreword. *Black Skin, White Masks.* By Frantz Fanon. Trans. Charles Lam Markmann. London: Pluto Press, 1967.

Cook, David and Michael Okenimpke. *Ngugi Wa Thiong'o: An Exploration of His Writings.* London: Heinemann, 1983.

Fanon, Frantz. *Black Skin, White Masks.* Trans. Charles Lam Markmann. London: Pluto Press, 1967.

Fanon, Frantz. *The Wretched of the Earth.* 1961. Trans. Constance Ferrington. London: Penguin, 1990.

Kenyatta, Jomo. *Facing Mount Kenya.* 1938. Nairobi: East African Educational Publishers, 1992.

Killam. G.D. *An Introduction to the Writings of Ngugi.* London: Heinemann, 1972.

Mukherjee, Meenakshi. "Beyond the Village." *Critical Essays on Indian Writing in English.* Ed. M.K. Naik, *et. al.*, Dharwar: Karnataka U, 1968.

Ngara, Emmanuel. "Ngugi Wa Thiong'o—*A Grain of Wheat.*" *Stylistic Criticism and the African Novel: A Study of the Language, Art Content of African Fiction.* London Heinemann, 1982.

Palmer, Eustace. *An Introduction to the African Novel.* London: Heinemann, 1972.

Rao, Damodar. Afterword. *Untouchable.* Mysore: Geetha Book House, 1995.

Rao, Damodar. "Social and Political Awareness in the Novels of Mulk Raj Anand and George Orwell." Diss. U of Mysore, 1979.

Robson, B. Clifford. *Ngugi Wa Thiong'o.* London: Heinemann, 1972.

Thiong'o, Ngugi wa. *A Grain of Wheat.* London: Heinemann, 1968.

Thiong'o, Ngugi wa. *Matigari.* 1987. Trans. Wangui Wa Goro. London: Heinemann, 1989.

Thiong'o, Ngugi wa. *Petals of Blood.* 1977. London: Heinemann, 1978.

Thiong'o, Ngugi wa. *The River Between.* 1965. London: Heinemann, 1981.

Thiong'o, Ngugi wa. *Weep Not, Child.* 1964. London: Heinemann, 1985.

A Land Like All The Others

5

War provides an excellent starting point from which to examine the relation between land and people in the novels of Anand and Ngugi. Both writers expose the pretensions of colonizing missions through arresting pictures of oppression by the colonizer not only in the colonies but in the colonizer's land. Anand and Ngugi were alert to the fact that the world wars had discovered the colonizers in the most uncomfortably ambiguous position. The labelling of the colonized as 'black' ('Kala admi') was in effect an attempt at discrediting native culture and civilization; yet, ironically, these 'savages' were called to fight in the wars "to save the British empire from defeat and collapse" (*Weep Not, Child*, 58), "to save the cause of civilization" (*Across the Black Waters*, 193). One of the Indian officers in Across the Black Waters aptly observes:

> They think we are all Gurkhas with Khukries in our mouths, savages who will creep up to them, take them by surprise and kill them. And the Sarkar is treating you as shock troops for that reason. Now you show them some of your savagery. All brave men like hand-to-hand fighting... you must charge the enemy with your bayonets, wherever you find him (127).

These peasants of the Indian sub-continent who were transplanted to the European war front knew not what shell fire or high explosives were; they called the war planes 'steel birds;' and were taught bayonet fighting only. Yet, they are asked to face the 'strangest weaponry!' The reader is made aware of a shocking paradox: on the one hand the colonial power encourages the Indian sepoys to prove their 'inherent savagery' against Germans; on the other, it preaches them 'peace' and 'love' at home (India)!

With great clarity Anand and Ngugi describe (in *Across the Black Waters*, *Petals of Blood* and *Weep Not, Child*) the conditions in which the natives went to fight their masters' wars. They are enticed, above everything else, by the masters' promise to reward the natives with their own (natives') land. Consideration of land becomes most important. For instance we read in *Across the Black Waters*:

> For when they first joined the army, these legionaries did so because, as the second, third or fourth sons of a peasant family overburdened with debt, they had to go and earn a little ready cash to pay off the interest on the mortgage of the few acres of land, the only thing which stood between the family and its fate... Besides, the soldier pledged to fight the battle of the King-Emperor, brought the necessary prestige to keep the policeman at bay and to bail out brothers, fathers and uncles who were arrested for non-payment of rent or debt (185).

What helps Anand and Ngugi in providing the right perspective to war is the agrarian background of native soldiers like Lalu, Kirpu (in *Across the Black Waters*) and Boro (in *Weep Not, Child*). Lalu, the protagonist of *Across the Black Waters*, is a peasant boy who pursues, like a number of other Indian peasants, a desperate and sterile quest across the waters. The factor that prompts Lalu and the host of farmers from remote Indian villages to turn soldiers in a war that does not concern them, and in a geography unknown to them, is their poverty. Famine, drought, moneylenders and heavy taxation by the government—these compel the humble folks to flee from their villages. In a bid to protect their lands from being auctioned and to save their families from starvation, disease and death, they join the army. The peasants are separated from their natural inheritance, *i.e.*, land. The King-Emperor's war causes the migration, displacement and alienation of the subjects. As Saros Cowasjee observes:

> The preservation of their own land, or a grant of piece of land for bravery by the Sarkar is what these peasants are fighting for. What greater irony than that these men should fight for a master who first takes away their land

> and reduces them to serfs and then urges them into battle with the promised land as gift (So Many Freedoms 111).

Anand's novel records the fate of such people: the soldiers return to their homes with the promised gifts as yet unrealized, and discover that their families have perished either because of famine or epidemic. Lalu's ambition was to reclaim the strip of his land that had been mortgaged: "When I come back, I shall ask the Karnal Sahib to order the bania to give back our mortgages, and to get the landlord to return the lands he has seized from us as a reward for fighting in this war" (205)—he expresses his hope in a letter from the Front to his mother. But on his return he finds his family destroyed, his mother and father dead, one of his brothers turned into a 'mystic Sadhu,' another sentenced to death, and his house and lands auctioned. In Lalu's tragedy lies the tragedy of the Indian village and Anand dramatizes a poignant truth: to disposes anyone of land is to deny him an identity. It is in this light that the reader empathizes with the soldier's desperate need to save his land at any cost.

If the villagers in Anand's novel travel from the corners of India it is in order to save an agrarian culture. Viewed this way, the image of 'Joan of Arc' ('Girl Jarnel' or girl general as Lalu calls her) becomes particularly relevant. The Indian peasant-soldiers are fascinated by the gigantic statue of Joan in Orleans. Lalu, the simple peasant lad from India, can esteem Joan of Arc through a similar figure in the history of his own land: that of the Queen of Jhansi who had fought the English to assert the rights of her people: "And the maid (Joan of Arc) seemed to become a heroine like the Rani of Jhansi. Lalu felt the blood coursing in his veins the ambition to follow her on the path of glory" (37).

Lalu's own life in a way is an enactment of Joan's. Joan, a village girl, daughter of an agriculturist, was a patriot and liberating force. Commanded by extraordinary visions she wielded the sword and drove the English colonizer out of France, but she was betrayed and burnt alive on false charges. Similarly, Lalu the peasant boy fights in the War to liberate his family and village from the monstrous forces of exploitation. And like Joan, he too is betrayed. Instead of securing a strip of land as he had dreamt all along, we learn in *The Sword and the Sickle* that Lalu becomes a suspect since he had been a German captive.

The peasants in *Weep Not, Child* are also motivated by similar hopes. They go to fight in World War II cherishing dreams that they would be rewarded with their own ancestral lands by the colonizer.

It is through these ordinary peasants that Ngugi and Anand render pictures of human excesses. The natives are bewildered by the sight of whites killing their own kind, and they doubt the 'superior wisdom' of the whites. Looking at the statue of Joan of Arc, Lalu narrates to other soldiers what he read as a school boy about the Hundred Year War: "Then, do you mean to say, that the Angrez Sahib and the Francisis were enemies at one time? One of the sepoys asked rather shocked. 'Yes,' Lalu answered, and continued his narrative while a whole group of sepoys clustered round him" (*Across the Black Waters*, 37).

Approaching the front, with the booming of guns over his head, Lalu finds his sense of sanity outraged by the killings:

> The element of sanity in Lalu persisted in the face of guns and in the face of the insanity, which had blown off the towers of the churches, and he could not believe that ordinary men and women of good sense, and the Governments of France, England and Germany, which were saner and wiser than the ordinary people over whom they ruled, could be engaged in a war in which men were being wounded and houses shattered (83).

The same bewilderment of the African is to be seen in Ngugi's world:

> Why should the white men have fought? Aaa! You could never tell what these people would do. In spite of the fact that they were all white, they killed one another with poison, fire and big bombs that destroyed the land.

> They have been called the black people to help them in killing one another (*Weep Not, Child,* 6).

We read in *Petals of Blood* that when the Europeans engaged in wars over the division of Africa, the small village of Ilmorog

> was a recruiting centre, and most young men were driven into the war with the butt end of the gun. Across the Ilmorog plains they went, clearing the roads, towards the Tanganyikan border to ferret out the Germans. Wonder of wonders: Wazungu were actually killing one another (122).

Ngugi and Anand depend on the unerring and sharp perceptions of the ordinary peasants to lay bare the immoderation in colonialism: whites kill whites. Shedding a drop of blood of any nationality amounts to shedding the blood of all human race: that is the profound truth that the rustic consciousness in these writers perceives. It is the same humanity the world over, and one land is like another. After arriving in France, Lalu wants to know if France is different from Hindustan. Stamping hard the ground, he asks Kirpu, "How do you like the land of France?" The amused reply from the elderly peasant-soldier is: "This land is like all the others, it came to be with the coming of life and will go down with death!" (12).

Young Lalu had his illusions. Before joining the army, he had imagined Europe or 'Vilayat' as a 'veritable heaven.' Likewise Njoroge (in *Weep Not, Child*) had thought England was the 'centre of all learning.' A common aspect of Ngugi's and Anand's vision is the disillusionment of the black colonized in Europe. A comparison of the barber's experience (in *Weep Not, Child*) with Lalu's (in *Across the Black Waters*) should bear this out. According to the barber, the First World War was a 'baby's war' compared to the Second, because the Africans who went to the First War "were only porters," but in the second one "we carried guns and we shot white men" (*Weep Not, Child,* 9). In *Across the Black Waters* too, there is such a feeling of power expressed by the Indian Lance-Naik Lok Nath. He instructs the sepoys thus:

> And I have always tried to instill in you the fact that as brave sepoys, you must charge the enemy without fear with your bayonets, wherever you find them and hit him in a vital spot. Aim at the heart, remember, the belly or the testicles of the enemy. If he has the advantage in attack, swiftly fell him with a blow from the butt end of your rifle and trample upon him and drive the bayonet deep into the body, and draw it out so that he bleeds and dies (127).

Allusions to the possibility of killing the whites in a neurotic expression of the desire in the oppressed class for equality. This also manifests as sexual desire. The barber in *Weep Not, Child* tells his people, "They (whites) are not the gods we had thought them to be. We even slept with their women" (9). And, of all the places, this was in Jerusalem! The Indian peasant boys in *Across the Black Waters* go through similar psychological states. Lalu once sights a few French girls; one of them "smiles coquettishly." Lalu turns round, "caressing the shapely contours of the girl's breasts, her hips and legs with a hunger that spread the panic abandon in his body" (38).

These descriptions remind one of Fanon's note on the black's hunger for dignity and equality in *Black Skin White Masks*:

> When my restless hands caress those white breasts, they grasp white civilization and dignity and make them mine (63).

It must be stressed that the vision of Anand and Ngugi saw as illusory, the desire to achieve equality and human dignity through sexual neuroses or through neurotic killing in a war. The barber (in *Weep Not, Child*) himself is aware of this, when he comments on the pleasure he derived from the white prostitutes. To a query, "How are they? (white women)" he replies: "Not different, Not different. I like a good fleshy black body with sweat. But they are... you know... so thin... without flesh... nothing" (9). "But it was wonderful to...", asks the listening voice, and the barber shatters the illusion before the query is fully articulated: "Well, before you started... you thought... it was eh—eh—wonderful. But after... it was nothing" (10).

Anand and Ngugi considered political problems not just in the colonial but in the total human context. In both we seen an unhesitating denunciation of war. The barber's talk in *Weep Not, Child* reminds Ngotho of

> His own travels and troubles during the First World War... His own two sons had also gone to this one (the Second World War). Only one had returned. And the one who had returned never talked much about the actual war, except to say that it had been a terrible waste of time (10).

Ngotho's attitude to war is more mature than the barber's. The criticism of war is dramatized more vividly and in greater detail in Anand's *Across the Black Waters* than in *Weep Not, Child.* As the Indian legionaries march through Marseilles, Orleans and Flanders to the Front, Lalu's vilayat turns out to be the Indian hell. The colour of the sky resembles the colour of the roof of hell. The trenches are akin to the descriptions of the Hindu hell. The sepoys are compelled to remain the dugouts, which are filled with muddy water due to incessant rains. The sepoys, isolated from one another, live in 'subterranean darkness'. Plagued by insects and lice and cold and hunger the sepoys trail through mud and marshes. And they are constantly exposed to the shelling of bombs. They are, in effect, transported to the netherworld:

> They had already come through the long and weary trail and were now in the stage of waiting in this visit, timeless universe for their doom to fulfill itself as if they had been suddenly transplanted into the world of their ancestors where men struggled against the elements of Gods and Destiny (*Across the Black Waters*, 118).

The entire battlefield changes into a vast graveyard: a netherworld populated by 'unhoused ghosts' and ruled by Yama, the God of Death. The soldiers from thousands of miles away suffer and die in a battle that has neither purpose nor meaning for them. Anand captures the exact picture of the battlefield through one of Lalu's nightmares:

> From the mud-walled cottages in the midst of a sea, which stank with a stagnant cream of green scum, appeared a woman with a naked coal black body, with eyes that glistened like burning stars and with a tongue that scattered sparks of fire, a sword in one of her ten hands and rifles in the others. And she stalked ruthlessly across the scrap heap, strewn with the butchered heads of goats... he stole a glance at her frightening glamour and knew it was Kali... There was a fissure in the field and out of it emerged rampaging hordes of demons, headed by Yama, the God of Death... The black woman... cut off her tongue with the sword, so that the blood dripped in a brook, which coloured the earth a deep crimson (135-36).

That a war is a monstrous betrayal of the energies of life is a truth grasped by the colonized who is deprived of land. Not that this truth in unavailable to the white man. It most certainly is. There is for example, Owen Sahib, the Adjutant, who is human enough to ask the native soldiers what they think of the War at a time when it is too risky to pose such a question to the 'obedient' soldiers. And Owen Sahib is displeased with the obsequious Sukhi Ram who utters, parrot-like, the colonizer's views on 'heroism' and 'saving the cause of civilization.' This English Officer has lost his best friend—an Indian—in the war, and has no illusions about the War. War, he says, is a meaningless waste. But he has not the same 'visionary power' in seeing what human costs are involved in the war. It is the villagers from far-away India, not the 'civilized' whites, who understand existentially, not just mentally, the conversion of land into a cemetery. This is seen with dramatic effect in an episode at the end of *Across the Black Waters.* A 'padre sahib' sermonizes to the soldiers about cherishing the "blessed hope of everlasting life." When he breaks off to chat informally with the Tommies, one of them asks, "How is life behind the lines, sir?" The Padre's answer runs thus:

> I only wish everyone could see what great care the chaplains of the Indian Army Corps are bestowing upon the little cemeteries in every part of France: each grave has its wooden cross with the name of the fallen soldier or officer inscribed on a tiny metal plate... And of course, the graves of many Indian officers and men, too, are cared for... (280).

Many Indian peasant-soldiers who do not understand English are curious to know from Lalu what the Padre had been saying. These are the men who have felt the full impact of the war at the front. And Lalu translates 'Affecting a pious face;' he mockingly begins to mime a prayer:

> Oh Lord Yessuh Missah (Jesus), we pray you to teach us to hate the enemy and help us to tear out his guts! We join our hands to you, and pray to you, son of God, intercede on our behalf to God who is your Father, to allot us nice graves with little brass plates with our names inscribed on them; we kneel before you and pray you to destroy the enemy (281).

The rustic lad Lalu translates in effect, the true meaning of the Padre's expression, 'everlasting life': War is a mad act that makes land a vast graveyard, a hell.

The traditional Hindu belief that crossing the sea is a sin appears to find justification, as Lalu recalls his mother's description of the various hells that sinners have to pass through:

> ... The hell where beings are cut, wounded and bruised by Yama and his hosts; the hell were reborn beings are struck down with blazing weapons, severed into pieces and left to rot in the mud and the slime; the hot and the cold hells; the hell where the sinners are crushed like sesame seeds; and the hell where they have to swim through oceanic expanses of dirty drains (155).

The protagonist's dreamy pictures of Europe as 'some heaven' receive severe jolts. The experience in actually makes him visualize the continent as a vast cemetery.

Anand's use of the image of the graveyard is crucial to the meaning of the novel. In the 'cause of civilization,' the European continent converts itself into an enormous graveyard. The smell of the burning flesh, the grey sky, darkness and the loneliness of the sepoys repeatedly emphasize the graveyard atmosphere. And the Indian soldiers, "isolated and apart they sat thus, these ghosts from another warmer world transplanted into this creeping wet cold autumnal underworld of Franceville" (141).

The image of the graveyard is used extensively in the novel. Every soldier feels threatened by a ghostly existence. For example, Daddy Dhanoo, a father-figure of Lalu, repeatedly insists on appropriate funeral rites after his death. In fact, his objection to coming to this war was that he might not receive the ceremonial rites. But when he dies in the drains with no rites, Lalu suffers from a terrible sense of guilt for not having been able to perform the last rites on Dhanoo's body. After all he was regarded as an adopted son by Dhanoo. Lalu moans in his dream:

> ... and yet the ghost of the corpse, became the spirit of Dhanoo, was pursuing him, for to his crazed brains it seemed as if the old man was following him about, chastising him, the adopted son, to offer the last rites on his body (154).

Lalu loses all his companions one by one becomes lonely. Their ghosts mingle with Yama's hordes and demand the lives of those who are alive. Thus, Lalu's angelic dreamland turns into a cemetery populated by malignant spirits.

Across the Black Waters is perhaps the only Indian English novel to have a First World War setting. As Alastair Niven points out, "Anand continues throughout *Across the Black Waters* to make a universal statement about the nature of war, apart from the particular tragedy of the Indian Sepoys in Flanders in 1914" (*The Yoke of Pity*, 70). It should be interesting to compare Anand's work with an Anglo-Indian novel having a similar World War I setting: John Masters' *The Ravi Lancers*. What distinguishes Anand from Masters is the formers' insight into the nature of the army that the King-Emperor has raised to nourish a war. The Indian contingent of the British army in *The Ravi Lancers* is a cavalry unit belonging to an Indian prince Major Krishna Ram, who is also the central character. Major Krishna Ram's dream is to win promotion as Brigadier General. Contrastively, we note in *Across the Black Waters,* that imperial England's regular infantry is drawn from the humblest regions of Indian society; a society that is frankly agrarian. Lalu is a peasant playing the role of a soldier, and his one ambition in life is to win a portion of his ancestral land as reward for his service. Unlike the English-educated Krishna Ram, Lalu is, to use Niven's expression, 'India's Everyman.'

Through an "Eastern Emplotment of the West" (as Dorothy Figuria puts it in her essay, "Mulk Raj Anand: Europe as an object of Orientalist Discourse") Anand expresses his primary concerns for what is essentially 'human.' At home, Lalu the young, rusting protagonist had regarded Europeans as "gods, distant and self-assured" (197). But in Europe he realizes that the whites too are people susceptible to sorrow and suffering and capable of finer human emotions like love, compassion and kindness. Not only the English and the French but even the Germans appear to him as human as Indians. This becomes most explicitly evident when the English and the German soldiers exchange Christmas greetings and distribute cakes in no-mans-land. The voyage across the waters to the European land enables the protagonist to have a vision of universal brotherhood, and in the course of the journey he understands that 'suffering humanity' is one. Now he can understand fully his officer's saying: "All the rules, the theorems, all the ideas—everything has been shattered in this war, buried in the mud" (194).

According to Clifford Robson, war is used by Ngugi "to puncture the notion of white superiority and infallibility by the introduction of stories about Africans killing white men and sleeping with white women" (*Ngugi Wa Thiong'o,* 28). This is only partly true. It is important to repeat that the humanist vision of Anand and Ngugi does not accommodate such illusory equations of power. Wanja's experience (in *Petals of Blood*) relating to her recapitulation of her family past may help understand this. There is in Petals of Blood a circumcision ceremony. An important part of the ritual is the preparation of Theng'eta, a drink distilled from a flower with red petals, 'petals of blood.' The flower of course is unique to the village of Ilmorog. The drink Theng'eta bares the soul, and after taking it, in a partly hallucinatory, partly trance-like state, Wanja reclaims her past. The minds eye opens to reveal her past. Her money-grabbing father had been to the Second World War, and her grandfather had gone to fight in the First. The scene that appears before her mind's eye is set in her mother's hut. The father is in army uniform and she sits on his knees, trying to spell words. It is necessary to quote the longish passage:

> 'Where have you been?' she asks him...
>
> 'Burma... India... Japan... lands far away, soldier fighting for the king.'
>
> 'Whom were you fighting?'
>
> 'Italians, Germans, Japanese.'
>
> 'You had a quarrel with them? Oh, you must have been angry.'
>
> 'Nop.'
>
> 'Why then were you fighting them?'
>
> 'A soldier does not ask questions... he obeys orders and dies, dies fighting for the king.'
>
> Which king? Does he also fight?
>
> 'Oh, stop it, little girl. You ask too many questions. Let's go play in the yard... soldier fighting for the king' (231-32).

Further, she sees that in the workshop her father is very nimble with his fingers when he works on the iron pipes. 'Oh father, where did you learn all this'? she asks. Her father replies: 'In the war, my daughter... a terrible waste of life... the bombs... the planes... these white men, my daughter, it is only human lives they cannot create. But I was only a soldier fighting for the king' (232). As the scene continues, Wanja sees her father quarreling with her mother. He has faith only in the power of money. His conviction is that only money can counter the imperial power of the English:

> 'I will tell you the secret of the white man's power: money. Money moves the world. Money is time. Money is beauty. Money is elegance. Money is power. Why, with money I can buy the princes of England... Money is freedom. With money we can bring light into darkness... Give me money and I can buy holiness and kindness and charity...' (233).

Exasperated, Wanja's mother cries:

> 'What money will make you traitor in this war?...
>
> You worship golden coins: It is God's image which is imprinted on the coins? A white God called George? and you killed. You murdered for white men.'
>
> 'That was different', says, her father.
>
> 'Different! Different! Is killing not killing? You were brave and strong to kill for the race of white people: didn't you retain a little courage, a little strength to lift a finger for your people, your clansmen? (233-34).

In either Ngugi's or Anand's world, it is the humanist voice that is dominant. It declares that humans are humans, irrespective of the colour of skin. Anand's allusion to the young writer's reaction to the European Crisis in the thirties is relevant here.

> All of us were united, wherever we were with thousands of others in the faith that we could defend the world heritage from the attacks of Germany, Italy and Japan as well as the reactionaries of our own countries... that we could help to achieve political and economic freedom for all and change our environment and ourselves in the process of this struggle (*Apology for Heroism*, 80).

The 'world heritage' is to be defended. When colonialism is compounded with war, the oppressor and the oppressed both can be bestialized. Anand and Ngugi would ascribe greater responsibility to the colonized to assert the human stature of mankind. This is the true significance of the native soldier fighting another's war in another land, hoping to get his own land from the colonizers as reward. This is why Anand does not allow his narrative, *Across the Black Waters* to lose itself in a cemetery world. In a world of nightmares, Lalu is allowed a healthy dream:

> ...And then she (Kali) shook the bells on her feet so that a great annihilation began, loud blares of trumpets, the banging of gongs, the drumming of drums. And the mud houses began to fall, the towers of huge buildings collapsed, the earth cracked and only a window remained through which a *green land* came to view (136) (Emphasis added).

Anand delicately balances the image of the green land against the image of the graveyard. The tender vision of a green land is but the farmer's village. The French farm-house by the brook where Lalu rests contains a hope of life. The death harboring Front is contrasted with the life-giving countryside of France. The village milieu in France enables Lalu to envision a hope for his village. His hope of reforming his village, getting his family out of debt and of increasing the yield of their land, takes a more definite shape. As Meenakshi Mukherjee puts it, Lalu's vague "idealism and desire to change his country... find a concrete basis in reality when he sees a French farm for the first time, notices the method of cultivation, the resulting prosperity" (95).

Lalu thinks that by adopting machines he can save his family from the exploitative system. The letter that Lalu writes to his mother from the billets is his passionate account of 'agrarian' France:

> This country is full of precious things such as machine ploughs, steel implements, sheep, pigs, cows, chickens... The Francis (Sic) of Franceville and the Flamands of Flanders are wonderful cultivators. They plough five times as much land in a day with tractor machine as we do in ten days with a wooden scratcher... The reason

> why these people are happier is because they do not borrow money from moneylenders, but from the bank at very low interest (205).

The sight of a clean, green, prosperous, French farm appeals immensely to Lalu. The French farmers' love of their land and livestock, their openness and friendliness greatly impresses him and establishes a bond of friendship between him and the French. Lalu can hope that this own village in India would testify to the reality of the Greenland whose vision he had in a French village.

An attempt to thwart the native's dream for his own land implies the violation of all that is human. Kiarie, the spokesman of the agitating masses in *Weep Not, Child* complains:

> Our fathers were taken captives in the first Big War to help in a war whose cause they never knew. And when they came back? Their land had been taken away for a settlement of the white soldiers... our people were taken and forced to work for these settlers. How could they have done otherwise when their land had been taken and they and their wives were required to pay heavy taxes to a government that was not theirs?... When the second Big War came, we were taken a fight Hitler—Hitler who had not wronged us. We were killed; we shed blood to save the British Empire from defeat and collapse (57-58).

War intensifies the tragedy in terms of deprivation of land. The tragedy is enacted in Ngotho's words too:

> It was the first big war. I was then young, a mere boy, although circumcised. All of us were taken by force. We made roads and cleared the forest to make it possible for the warring white man to move more quickly. The war ended... But Ngo! The land was gone. My father and many others had been removed from our ancestral lands. He died lonely, a poor man waiting for the white man to go (*Weep Not, Child*, 25).

If the humanity of the ordinary villagers in the worlds of Anand and Ngugi is appealing, it is because land is such a need as to prompt them to undertake a trip to Inferno, which is what war-ridden Europe is. The predicament is described most poignantly by Anand:

> Sometimes a war was on somewhere, in a geography of which the family or the son had no conception, and he faded out into thin air only to confirm his own and the family's prejudice that all who went beyond the mountains or across the black waters were destined for hell (*Across the Black Waters,* 186).

In both Anand and Ngugi landlessness (*i.e.,* not having one's ancestral land) corresponds to meaninglessness, as terrible as hell. One lives meaningfully when one dies on his own land. Nyakinyua in *Petals of Blood* is such a character. The stature of this mother-figure is the loftiest in the novel (with "deep lines in her face" she is "beautiful even in age"). She is the spirit that guides the villagers of Ilmorog and she talks to the villagers "as if she had been everywhere, as if she had actually participated in the war against Germans" (123). When the neo-colonial situation in the novel deprives the natives of Ilmorog of their land, old Nyakinyua tries to urge the villagers to make a fight. "She had said that she could not even think of being buried in somebody else's land. For what would her man say to her when she met him on the other side?" (*Petals of Blood,* 176). She dies peacefully in her sleep before she can be dispossessed of her land. Here is a life well lived.

Not only do Anand and Ngugi employ war in their fiction to expose the colonizers' transgressions but also to affirm the nationalist aspirations of the colonized. One comes across in their works, references to people who return from foreign lands with ideas of liberty. The common villagers without actually participating in the distant wars, do understand through the accounts of those who had gone out, what the European wars imply. This is the dominant atmosphere in *The Sword and the Sickle* and *A Grain of Wheat.* Both novels deal with national movements. People's memories of the Second War are quite vivid when Emergency is imposed at eruption of the Mau-Mau Movement in *A Grain of Wheat*:

> One day people in Thabai and Rung'ei woke up to find themselves ringed around with black and white soldiers carrying guns, and tanks last seen on the road during Chruchill's war with Hitler. Gunfire smoked in the sky, people held their stomachs. Some men locked themselves in latrines; others hid among the sacks of sugar and beans in the shops. Yet others tried to sneak out of the town towards the forest, only to find that all roads to freedom were blocked (7).

The First War in *The Sword and the Sickle* and *A Grain of Wheat* has made the peasants indignant:

> Soldiers came back from the war and told stories of what they had seen in Burma, Egypt, Palestine and India; wasn't Mahatma Gandhi, the saint, leading the Indian people against British rule? Kihika fed on these stories... (*A Grain of Wheat*, 97).
>
> Comrade Lal Singh has spoken of the war in which he fought with other Hindustani sepoys and goras, where lakhs of men were killed and which brought famine to Hindustan... to be sure, Comrade Lal Singh is right: the poor soldiers get killed for the glory of their Sarkars. To be sure, the people of one country have no quarrel with those another...
>
> As Comrade Lal Singh says, there are two races and two religions in the world; the rich and the poor. That is so all over the world, for all the folk who have gone to Vilayat tell the same tale: there are gora coolies and sweepers and there are rich Sahibs (*The Sword and the Sickle*, 347).

A Grain of Wheat deals with Kenya's liberation and the transfer of power from the British to Kenyan people, *The Sword and the Sickle*, which also deals with the liberation struggle of India does not show the successful completion of the struggle. But this must not prevent us from seeing how alike Anand and Ngugi are in their perceptions. In both novels doubts regarding substantial difference between Independence and Post-Independence periods prevail. The two writers see the same conditions in the pre-Independence and post-Independence periods of their countries. In *The Sword and the Sickle*, Razwi, a revolutionary and an important spokesman of Anand, prophesies:

> When the Badeshi state goes, there will be a Swadeshi State—a mere change of names and labels! For, I believe they will ever sack the I.C.S. personnel, reduce their pay or cut their pensions. And, what's more, I believe they will use the same police, which now beat them with staves, and the same regulations by which they are put in goals, to suppress those whom they don't like! (331).

This is comparable to the apprehensions of the anxious people in *A Grain of Wheat*. On the Uhuru Day, the crowd ponders:

> Would the government now become less stringent on those who could not pay tax? Would there be more jobs? Would there be more lands? (245).

Gikonyo, one of the protagonists, expresses the same doubts: "Would Uhuru bring the land to African hand?" (181).

One has to compare the descriptions of the "New" Ilmorog in *Petals of Blood* to see Ngugi has no illusions of an independence that only substitutes the neo-colonial for the colonial. The beneficiaries in the changed system are the ones who had exploited the children of the soil in the old system. A bitter Wanja tells Karega:

> Kimeria, who had his fortune as a Home Guard transporting bodies of Mau-Mau killed by the British, was still prospering... Kimeria, who had ruined my life and later humiliated me by making me sleep with him during our journey to the city... this same Kimeria was one of those who would benefit from the new economic progress of Ilmorog (*Petals of Blood*, 293).

In the New Ilmorog, the land is going out of African hand. Karega says,

> The company's sugar plantation was started soon after Independence... to develop the area... to raise the standard of living. A number of peasants who were

> driven off the land were encouraged to grow sugar on their plots instead of food (*Petals of Blood*, 289).

Money reigns supreme in New Ilmorog. Culture is most blatantly on sale. Women "sing native songs and dance for white tourists... they are paid well" says Wanja (*Petals of Blood*, 292). "Nothing is free" in New Ilmorog, she tells Munira who had been her close associate for a long time, and charges him money for getting into bed with her:

> 'This is New Kenya. You want it, you pay for it, for the bed and the light and my time and the drink that I shall later give you and the breakfast tomorrow. All for a hundred Shillings. For you. Because of old times. For others it will be more expensive' (*Petals of Blood*, 279).

In *The Sword and the Sickle*, independence is not achieved, and hence there is no actual picture of a neo-colonial system. Yet, there is a similar sensitive grasp of the growing influence of money:

> Suddenly it occurred... the impact of that misery and poverty which the 'money famine' had started in India during his absence in the war and which seemed even more intense in the small towns than it was in the villages, because of the migration of the poorest peasants townwards. Something so terrible and catastrophic had happened during the war that though he could not even yet grasp it in all its immense possibilities... as it had been before (362).

The Sword and the Sickle and *A Grain of Wheat* do not end on a negative note, however. The faith that Anand and Ngugi repose in humanity makes them keep alive the dream of a 'human' existence for mankind. That dream is not stained by romanticism, since what is shown as a value to be aspired is the family-unit in society. By making their heroes return to the love and duties of family (as can be seen in Gikonyo's and Lalu's case) both writers demonstrate that the survival of familial relationships are fundamental to a greater human happiness. *A Grain of Wheat* ends with the re-union of Gikonyo and Mumbi (reminiscent of the legendary

Gikuyu-Mumbi, founders of the Gikuyu tribe) and with Gikoyno's reverie:

> He thought about the wedding gift, a stool carved from Muiri wood. 'I'll change the woman's figure. I shall curve a woman big-big with child' (280).

Anand's novel similarly closes with Lalu's contemplation of his re-union with family:

> Lalu felt easier now that the night was over. He rubbed his eyes and stared about him. He must get ready for the day. He must remember to send a message to Maya to ask her how their new-born son was getting on, though from her answer to his previous inquiries during her pregnancy, he knew what she would say:
>
> 'Sardar Lal Singh, your child is alive and kicking!' (386).

In their worlds populated by revolutionaries, soldiers, capitalists and landlords, both Anand and Ngugi uphold the wisdom of the simple villager. The concern for family at the close of The Sword and the Sickle and A Grain of Wheat testifies to this. The peasant's wisdom recognizes the priority of what is human. Uncle Kirpu's comment in Across the Black Waters best summarizes that wisdom:

> This land (France)... is like all the others, it came to be with the coming of life and will go down with it (12).

WORKS CITED

Anand, Mulk Raj. *Across the Black Waters.* 1940. Bombay: Popular-Kutub, 1955.

Anand, Mulk Raj. *Apology for Heroism.* 1946. Bombay: Popular-Kutub, 1980.

Anand, Mulk Raj. *The Sword and the Sickle.* 1942. New Delhi: Arnold-Hienemann, 1984.

Cowasjee, Saros. *So Many Freedoms.* New Delhi: OUP, 1977.

Fanon, Frantz. *Black Skin, White Masks.* Trans. Charles Lam Markmann. London: Pluto Press, 1967.

Figuria, Dorothy. "Mulk Raj Anand: Europe as an Object of Orientalist Discourse." South Asian Review. 15:12, July 1991.

Mukherjee, Meenakshi, "Beyond the Village." *Critical Essays on Indian Writing in English*. Ed. M.K. Naik, *et al.* Dharwar, India: Karnataka UP, 1968.

Niven, Alastair. *The Yoke of Pity: A Study in the Fictional Writings of Mulk Raj Anand*. New Delhi: Arnold-Heinemann, 1978.

Robson, B. Clifford. *Ngugi Wa Thiong'o*. London: Heinemann, 1972.

Thiong'o, Ngugi wa. A Grain of Wheat. London: Heinemann, 1968.

Thiong'o, Ngugi wa. *Petals of Blood*. 1977. London: Heinemann, 1978.

Thiong'o, Ngugi wa. *Weep Not, Child*. 1964. London: Heinemann, 1985.

Conclusion

6

The literary output of each of the two writers here studied is immense. The fact that they very prolific must not make us forget the severe challenges they had to face when they started to write. Both wrote 'protest' literature. Their books did embarrass at times the political establishments. Both had to define the realm in which the novel was to operate in their lands. The challenge was to uphold the relevance of non-Eurocentric models against the Eurocentric. This had to be achieved by relating their own traditions to modern experience. As Ngugi puts it in *Decolonizing the Mind.*

> Amidst massive illiteracy, amidst the conflicting phonetic systems even within the same language, amidst the new superstitions of the bible and the church, how can we talk meaningfully of the African novel? How could I contemplate the novel as a means of my reconnection with the people I left behind? My targeted audience—the people—were the two classes represented by Kamiriithu. How could I take a form so specifically bourgeois in its origins, authorship and consumption, for such a reconnection with a populace ridden with the problems outlined above? (67-68).

Both writers dealt with this problem by conceiving their writings within the context of a world heritage. Ngugi says:

> The social or even national basis of the origins of an important discovery or any invention is not necessarily a determinant of the use to which it can be put by its inheritors... Gunpowder was invented in China. It was effectively used by the European bourgeoisie in its spread and expansion to all the concerns of the globe.

> Mathematical science was invented by the Arabs but it has been appropriated by all the nations of the earth. The history of science and technology taken as a whole is a result of contributions from many nations and races in Africa, Asia, Europe, America and Australia. The same is true of the history of the arts—music, dance, sculpture, paintings and literature (*Decolonizing the Mind*, 68).

It is this total human context in which Anand too places himself as a writer:

> As the novel concerns the whole of human life, in all its multifarious expression,... we must remember the truism that all art forms of every period more or less reflect the environment, either by extending the accepted tradition with its old myths,... or by moulding the environment, much, or little, ... or by revolutionizing it so as to cohere with the new myths which dimly grow from the hunches about ourselves (Indian Literature of the Past Fifty Years, 110-111).

The most important factor in the total human context, for both writers, are the common labourer and the peasant. With great conviction and clarity Ngugi speaks of the cultural achievement in the world:

> The most important breakthroughs in music, dance and literature have been borrowed from the peasantry. Even the games like football and athletics have come from ordinary people while all the others normally associated with the upper classes were refinements of those of the people. Nowhere is this more clear than in the area of languages. It is the peasantry and the working class who are changing language all the time in pronunciations, in forming new dialects, new words, new phrases and new expressions. In the hands of the peasantry and the working class, language is changing all the time, it is never at a standstill (*Decolonizing the Mind*, 68).

When in detention, Ngugi contemplated seriously on the appropriate 'fiction language,' that is, 'fiction itself as language'

(*Decolonizing the Mind*, 75). He felt compelled from within to write in Gikuyu.

Mulk Raj Anand, whose ideas about the dynamics of creation are similar to Ngugi's, did not switch over from English to Punjabi or any other 'Indian' language. But he is as much concerned about his readership. It is most important for him to relate to his audience, and the language that can be heard by the common man is the right language, according to him. In India where there are numerous languages, English got peculiarly assimilated by Indian culture. The English that Anand uses in his fiction is certainly not British English. In any case, for both Anand and Ngugi, content is the ultimate arbiter of form and language.

This thesis ends with the hope that further exploration in the field would be rewarding. An examination of Anand and Ngugi from the Marxian angle could be attempted. Also, the nature of violence in their fictional works appear to be a probe worthy subject. Towards the end of *Matigari*, which has a neo-colonial setting, the crowd burns the houses and property of the rich and the hero returns to the forest (from which he emerged at the beginning), and prophesies a 'Second Coming' of the Mau-Mau struggle. The language here is reminiscent of Fanon's:

> Justice for the oppressed springs from the organized armed power of the people. Matigari had already laid down the belt of peace. He would now return to the forests and wear his belt of arms for a second struggle (*Matigari*, 160).

Devil on the Cross ends with the murders of the 'rich old man from Nakuru' and his two rich associates. With a sense of poetic justice, Waringa the protagonist shoots down her seducer and the exploiters and walks off the scene in a triumphant manner. Similarly, Wanja, one of the protagonists of *Petals of Blood* kills the representatives of neo-colonialism. In *The Sword and the Sickle* there is Razwi, who is spokesman for violence. Professor Verma and Count Kanwar Rampal Singh counter his arguments for violent means to achieve freedom, but the interesting fact is that Razwi remains the character with vitality. There are other advocates of violence in Anand's world like Sauda, the trade union member, and Ratan in *Coolie.* P.K. Rajan's observation is worth consideration:

> Violence, in Anand's novel... has its distinctive dualism. He shows his awareness that positive revolutionary movements cannot avoid violence, but the possibility of having violence without murder seems to obsess his humanist imagination—an obsession which it (sic) has remained impossible for him to overcome (*Mulk Raj Anand: A Revaluation,* 177).

It must be clarified that both Anand and Ngugi were committed to humanitarian vision of society. Ngugi believes that

> We must all struggle for a world in which one's cleanliness is not depended on another's dirt, one's health on another's ill-health, and one's welfare on another's misery (*Barrel of a Pen: Resistance to Repression in Neo-Colonial Kenya,* 75).

Anand declares, "violence against violence is futile" (*The Hindu,* May 9, 1993).

In the present comparative study the parallels between Anand and Ngugi may appear too neat. One reason for such an approach is obviously the anxiety to assert, in the absence of comparative studies of the two writers, their literary kinship. The interaction between past and present is a compelling aspect of Anand's and Ngugi's attempts to relate their traditions to modern experience; and since it is easy to see a dichotomy between the traditional and the modern in protest literatures of the colonized regions, there was the need to guard, from the very beginning, against the dangers of making the tradition-modernity polarity simplistic. Therefore, the two writers are discussed, not individually, but in an inter-related manner throughout. Since the thesis is mainly interpretative, frequent citations and quotations from primary sources became necessary.

WORKS CITED

Anand, Mulk Raj. "Old Myth—New Myth: Recital Versus Novel." *Indian Literature of the Past Fifty Years*. Ed. C.D. Narasimhaiah. Mysore: U of Mysore, 1970.

Anand, Mulk Raj. *"On Power and Violence."* The Hindu. January 17, 1993.

Anand, Mulk Raj. *The Sword and the Sickle*. 1942. New Delhi: Arnold Publishers, 1984.

Rajan, P.K. *Mulk Raj Anand: A Revaluation*. New Delhi: Arnold Associates, 1995.

Thiong'o, Ngugi wa. *Barrel of a Pen: Resistance to Repression in Neo-Colonial Kenya*. Trenton N.J. African World Press, 1985.

Thiong'o, Ngugi wa. *Decolonizing the Mind: The Politics of Language in African Literature*. 1986. London: James Currey, 1987.

Thiong'o, Ngugi wa. *Devil on the Cross*. 1982. Trans. Ngugi wa Thiong'o. London: Heinemann, 1987.

Thiong'o, Ngugi wa. *Matigari*. 1987. Trans. Wangui wa Goro. London: Heinemann, 1989.

Thiong'o, Ngugi wa. *Moving the Centre: The Struggle for Cultural Freedoms*. London: James Currey, 1993.

Thiong'o, Ngugi wa. *Petals of Blood*. 1977. London: Heinemann, 1987.

Appendices

APPENDIX—A

INTERVIEW WITH NGUGI WA THIONG'O

Lingaraja Gandhi: Professor Ngugi, I have undertaken a Comparative Study of your writing with Mulk Raj Anand of India who championed the cause of 'low dregs of humanity' in his writings. Anand, a "precursor of Frantz Fanon" published his seminal work *Untouchable* in 1935. And, his major novels were published when India was still a colony of Britain. Are you, by any means aware of his works?

Ngugi: A comparative study of Anand's work and my own would be very interesting. I have read his works, particularly his *Coolie*, and I believe all his three works (*Untouchable, Coolie* and *The Village*) were taught at the Literature Department, University of Nairobi, in the 70's when I was the chairman of the department. This was a result of the changes in the re-organization of the teaching of literature at the University following the debate, which was initiated by the call for the abolition of the English Department. (See my book, *Homecoming* and *Decolonizing the Mind*). I have met him, many years ago, at an Afro-Asian writers' Conference in Beirut, Lebanon, in or about 1966. Kenya and India share so much because of the many years of historical contact as well as being colonized by the same power and of course Kenya having a large part of her citizenry from India. There is of course the impact of the independence of India on Kenyan and African anti-colonial nationalism after the Second World War.

LG: In *Weep Not, Child* and *A Grain of Wheat,* you present Gandhi as a crusader of freedom and a liberating force. Is your admiration of Gandhi consistent with your appreciation of the Marxist—Fanonist position?

Ngugi: We saw Mahatma Gandhi as the symbol of Indian resistance to British rule. His anti-colonialism, his affirmation of Indian identity, and his crusade for independence are not inconsistent with any anti-colonial, anti-imperialist position of theories of national and class liberation.

LG: The Indian settler community in East Africa, through its allied activities in business, Trade Unions and Journalism fought against Colonial government's repressive measures and generated among Africans the National consciousness. The Indian-Kenyan leaders like Makham Singh, Pandya, A.B. Patel, Pinto, D'Souza, Jaswant Singh, among many others have contributed to East African political awareness. [Robert Gregory's book, *Asian Politics in East Africa* 1900-1967. (India: Orient Longman), 1993 apprises about this]. After Indian Independence, the Indian Government supported African cause. But in your fictional and non-fictional works, you don't refer to India's support for African liberation. May I know the reason?

Ngugi: Surely you must have read my prison memoirs: *Detained: A Writer's Prison Dairy.* I have placed Makhan Singh, Gama Pinto, etc., in the center of the anti-colonial struggles in Kenya.

LG: Kenyan communities (ethnic groups) other than your own Gikuyu, do not figure prominently in your writings. Is this the reason why some critics perceive you as a Gikuyu chauvinist?

Ngugi: I look at Kenya and history from the class standpoint of the worker and peasant. What I say of the two classes, no matter their specific regional location is by extension applicable to the two classes on the national and Pan-African scale.

LG: All your novels are written after Kenyan Independence. But the novels set in pre-independent Kenya suggest the assimilation of the old and the new—the traditional and the Colonial (modern)—values and cultures, whereas the novels set in post-independent Kenya call for the total rejection of imperial tradition and for re-structuring of society based on indigenous languages and cultures. What are the compulsions behind such a changed attitude?

Ngugi: As a matter of fact both *The River Between* and *Weep Not, Child* were written and finished between 1961 and 1963. It's only that they were published after 1963. The two novels mentioned are set in pre-independent Kenya. I do not accept your equation of the colonial with the modern. The most modern thing about Kenya were the anti-colonial resistance and the skills and values it generated and embodied. The novels that follow these two are however have more clear about base of both imperialist dominance and anti-imperialist resistance. That's the difference. An ideological shift in class perspective. There is in the latter works a more consistent identification with the position of the workers and the peasant.

LG: Why is the novel a major form in the Third World Literature specially with the writers dealing with social and political issues?

Ngugi: The novel is essentially a continuation of the ancient storytelling traditions of most peoples in the world.

LG: What are the special challenges of African (and particularly Kenyan) writers of novels in English?... This was in a context when there was no tradition of novel.

Ngugi: I really have dealt with the language question in my books, *Decolonizing the Mind* and *Moving the Centre.* See also the forthcoming books *Writers in Politics* (Revised edition, James Curry Ltd., 1997): *Penpoints Gunpoints and Dreams: The Performance of Literature and Power in Post-colonial Africa* (Oxford University Press, 1997).

LG: In most of your novels and short stories you make young boys protagonists. May I now the reasons for the selection of young characters as heroes? How it helps you dramatize the reality you want to?

Ngugi: The young embody the to-marrow of any community.

LG: Eustace Palmer observes that "the main weakness of *Weep Not, Child* is the choice of Njoroge as the central consciousness... One could hardly expect him to understand the complexity of national affairs. The same tendency in an adult would have been much more convincing". Would you like to respond to this criticism?

Ngugi: If there are weakness, they have nothing to do with the choice of Njoroge as the central consciousness. The critic should identify what he considers be weaknesses and if true try to account for them.

LG: Why are many of your protagonists drawn form peasant stock?

Ngugi: Peasant and worker. The two classes form the social majority in Africa. They are also the most productive while being the most exploited in both colonial and post-colonial Kenya. Hence their role is emphasized.

APPENDIX—B

CONVERSATIONS WITH MULK RAJ ANAND

— Lingaraja Gandhi
6-7 August, 1996, Bombay

LG: Sir, Your literary career covers three phases of modern Indian life, namely—the pre-Independent, the transitional and the post Independent. In other words, you have written both in colonial and neocolonial periods, and you have given expression to the implications of British Colonialism in your fictional and non-fictional works. Working in such varying contexts, what were the 'special' challenges that you faced as an Indian English novelist? And, how different are the problems of a writer of the "Thirties" from those who wrote subsequently?

MRA: Before the 'thirties' the example of Tagore was there. Tagore gave up his 'knighthood,' which was a very important act. His "Hindustan Hamara" was there before us. The Tagore family came to nationalism radically only after 1919. Tagore's novel *Gora*, reflects the nationalist concerns of the twentieth century and his *Ghare Baire* is written in the stream of consciousness technique. Tagore's contemporaries and immediate successors—Sharat Chandra, Tara Shankar Bandhopadyay, Bidhuti Bhusan, Premchand were equally committed to the humanitarian vision of society. Before Tagore, Bankim wrote *Anand Math*, the first novel of India's early struggle for Independence. The freedom movement was the major concern before 1947.

LG: Do you see any direct relationship between rise of the novel in India and Indian nationalism?

MRA: Any book or novel has to deal with the time—the situation of the time, about the human situation, political situation, social situation of the time. This was the reason why even a non-committed writer like R.K. Narayan had to do the novel *Waiting For the Mahatma*. He didn't go to jail, we did. What is going on can't be ignored. There was a movement going on. He had to do the novel *Waiting For the Mahatma*. No one can evade the consequences of the time. No committed, sincere writer of Africa, Asia and Latin America can afford to remain non-political, apolitical.

Fundamentally no creative writer of his time could probably evade the happenings of his time. Beginning with *Mahabharat*, which is about the war of Pandavas and Kauravas—a political war, which is relevant to our situation, today. All fiction, all writing except the Shastras are political in nature and have social purpose in mind. In *Mahabharat* one sees the model novel of the world. Without *Mahabharat*, there is no Mulk Raj Anand or R.K. Narayan or Raja Rao. All our writing is in the tradition of *Mahabharat*. The Indian writer is writing *Mahabharat* all the time. All the problems that we are dealing with today have been dealt in *Mahabharat.* Whatever Indian languages you write in today—Oriya, Gujrati, Assamee, Malayalam—all (works) are part of the novel called *Mahabharat.* There is only one novel that is *Mahabharat.*

The language of *Mahabharat* was the language of the time; no written language, but spoken, understood by the people. All our themes have to be taken from *Mahabharat.* Tagore has said this. Dandin's novel, *Ten Princes* of the 15th century is the only novel after *Mahabharat,* which doesn't take theme from the epic.

LG: Why is novel a major form in Third World Literature, specially with the writers dealing with social and political issues?

MRA: Inevitable.

LG: You broke ground in fictional tradition—East or West, by choosing the subject matter that had never entered the realm of 'Polite Literature' (to use your phrase) and by making a scavenger the protagonist in your seminal work *Untouchable.* But, you wrote in a language that is not spoken or understood by the people about whom it was written. In a world where the debate concerning the writer and his audience is gaining importance it would be interesting to know how you view on author-audience relation?

MRA: My language is Punjabi. I mean, I translate from Punjabi into English. I feel in Punjabi. No one can say I am not influenced by English language. At that time, no language of India except Bengali was ripe enough to write a novel. My novel—whether it has reached the actual audience or not—it doesn't matter. It has reached the audience capable of taking it. My audience is just not confined to Punjab. The total numbers of copies of my novel (Untouchable) sold in Punjab were only 200 copies.

Don't take language chauvinism as the only case for derison. At the moment, bring to me some Indian writers who write in German, French, Italian, Russian languages about India. They don't know what to do. They are bankrupt. Bankruptcy is no answer. V.K. Gokak, Shivaram Karanth authentically write in Kannada.

I can't wish away Raja Rao. Until *Kanthapura* there was no novel in Kannada. *Kanthapura* is the only novel in Kannada, which is significant to Kannada language or English. Because, Raja Rao knew the narrative form and the folk of Karnataka. I don't force Indian people to write in English when they don't have the talent to write. Raja Rao turned up, I welcomed him. He is the most significant writer of India—even beyond me. Raja Rao's novel is a very important novel of a period of India—the Gandhian period. *Kanthapura* is in English. Why didn't he write in Kannada? Why? I don't care a damn in what language he wrote it, so long as he wrote employing the right technique in the novel form. We are all part of *Mahabharat* novel. *Mahabharat* is being written in many languages now—not only in English. Don't reject episodes of *Mahabharat.* R.K. Narayan, Mulk Raj Anand we all are writing *Mahabharat.*

LG: In a number of your novels and short stories you make young boys protagonists. What are the reasons for your selecting young characters as heroes? Or how does it help you to dramatize the reality you want to?

MRA: Because, I saw in the young the future of India.

LG: Why are many of your protagonists drawn from the peasant stock?

MRA: I know the peasants of Punjab well. I am fond of them. They are very vital people. They are genuinely human compared to the caste Hindus. The Sikhs are anti-caste people.

LG: Your portrayal Gandhi in *Untouchable* differs considerably from that in *The Sword and the Sickle.* You render Gandhi as saint in *Untouchable* and in *The Sword and the Sickle* you almost caricature him. What are the compulsions behind the changed attitude towards Gandhi?

MRA: In *Untouchable* Gandhi is being seen as the emancipator of untouchables. He calls the untouchables Harijan, the children of God, to whom I went myself and wrote the novel. In *The Sword and the Sickle* there is a man, a peasant leader who goes to Gandhi. As a leader he wants Gandhi to do something for the peasantry and Gandhi doesn't. The hero remarks about Gandhi's ears. That is because he thinks Gandhi is not listening to him. He feels strongly about Gandhi... I am only recording what happened.

I am not using Gandhi either in favour or against. I am only dictating about the time. Gandhi to me represents a whole era. He is a hero of our time and sometimes, no hero.

LG: Your books are interpreted in broadly three ways. You are read as: (1) a humanist (Balaram Gupta's (*Mulk Raj Anand: A Study in Humanist Perspective*, 1974); (2) a progressive Marxist line of thinker (Ambuj Kumar Sharma's *The Theme of Exploitation*, 1992) and (3) an ambivalent writer, belonging to both Gandhian humanism and Marxian socialism (P.K. Rajan's *Mulk Raj Anand: A Revaluation*, 1995). Where do you like to place yourself?

MRA: I belong to all the three places you mentioned.

LG: From peasants and workers of early novels, you shift the attention to the prince in the *Private Life of An Indian Prince* and you successfully win the reader's sympathy for the prince. Did you think that the struggles of the proletariat (you portrayed in early novels) were over?

MRA: My concern is with the whole of life. I include in this novel—maid servants, Parsee gentlemen, Queen Victoria, Princes of India, peasants of Punjab, Rickshaw drivers of Calcutta... My view is comprehensive. The novel even gives the picture of the working class of London. In this story of mine, I have shown the prince (whom I knew personally) who didn't want to join the Indian union and who fell in love with a nymphomaniac. As a result of Permanent Settlement Act, the prince wanted to own the land but Sardar Vallabh Bhai Patel (then Home Minister of India) forced him to join the nation.

LG: A post-colonial critic points out that you are a writer of middle class interests (Arun P. Mukherjee, "Exclusions of Post-Colonial Theory and *Untouchable*: A Case Study," Ariel, 1991). She alleges that in *Untouchable* you (a) deny power, agency and political action to the hero, (b) and that the Dalit movements, which were already active are hidden from the text; and that (c) you allow the middle class voices (Poet, Barrister and Gandhi) to prevail at the end. As such the text fails to provide leadership to the oppressed class. How do you respond to this criticism?

MRA: I only say, behind this novel of mine—which is called the 'creative manifesto of Dalits in India'—there is Thomas Paine. And Ambedkar would not have been what he was if he had not read Thomas Paine, who wrote *The Rights of Man*.

APPENDIX—C

LETTERS FROM MULK RAJ ANAND

LETTER—1

Mulk Raj Anand,
#25, Cuffe Parade,
Bombay-400005.
Phone Res: 2181371
18-9-95

Dear Shri Lingaraja Gandhi,

I am reassured by your note of 6th September in which you have revealed that you have written about the novel, *Across the Black Waters*.

After three reviews by military men when the novel appeared, the literary intelligentsia had nothing about this important book of mine.

I find our colleagues hidebound in their own 'bhasha' atmosphere, without realizing the significance of fictions, which have relevance to international history.

Actually, recently, in a Seminar in Johnstown University organized by Dr. K.D. Verma, an American teacher, Dorothy Figuria, has written an intensive analysis of *Across the Black Waters*. It is entitled 'Europe as an object of orientalist discourse'. It is intensive in its search for meanings and implications. I am sending you a Xeroxed copy.

I feel, that few professors in English literature understand that, from my long stay in the west, I had the advantage of participation in the world debate about the First World War. And like Henri Barbusse's novel *Under Fire* and *All Quiet On The Western Front* as also Robert Graves *Goodbye To All That*, my novel, was reckoned as a frontline recreation of a unique phenomena, the decimation of Indian troops in a war, which was claimed to be for freedom—but involved as canon fodder, soldiers, who not free as their country was under British Colonial domination.

In order to understand the implications of *Across the Black Waters*, you might like to read, *Culture and Imperialism* by Edward Said, which more than any other book recreates the colonial contempt for human rights, which the Imperialists indulge in for five hundred years. And which long period was upturned only by the intense struggle of our people for a hundred years or more.

I am sending you the American essay, which I feel, might help your own perceptions.

I am reassured about your other project Comparative Study of Ngugi Wa Thiong'o and Mulk Raj Anand.

I know Achebe's novels but not Thiong'o's. Are they available anywhere in India?

Regards,

Lingaraja Gandhi,
No. 231, I Main, Jayalakshmipuram,
Mysore-570012. India.

Sincerely
(Mulk Raj Anand)

LETTER—2

Mulk Raj Anand,
#25, Cuffe Parade,
Bombay-400005.
Phone Res: 2181371

8-10-95

Dear Friend, Lingraj Gandhi,

On my return from Delhi, I have seen your note of 27th September.

I apologize for not commenting on your paper about *Across the Black Waters.*

I have read it again and find that it is very perceptive and very near the essay submitted by Dorothy Figuria on *Across the Black Waters*: "*Europe as an Object of Orientalist Discourse.*"

I am sending you a Xeroxed copy of that paper.

Only one background reference is missing in both the papers, which could have occurred to you as an Indian that *Across the Black Waters* may be a short book of the Mahabharat's being written all over the world by various writers all showing that in a war everyone dies and few survive.

As an Indian novel, I had in mind to do this novel, as a contemporary expression of the theme that violence against violence is ultimately futile; and the only person who perceived this truth and propagate it in our time was Mahatma Gandhi.

I am grateful for your information about the African novelist Ngugi. Perhaps I can borrow one or two of his novels, while I will try to acquire them through friends in America.

I know the works of Achebe and Wole Soyinka but not Ngugi.

Regards,

Lingaraja Gandhi,
No. 231, I Main,
Jayalakshmipuram,
Mysore-570012. India.

Sincerely
(Mulk Raj Anand)

LETTER—3

Mulk Raj Anand,
#25, Cuffe Parade,
Bombay-400005.
Phone Res: 2181371

14-2-96

Dear Shri Lingaraj Gandhi,

Greetings !

Please forgive the delay in writing back in answer to your note of 12th December. I have been away from home.

In your possible review of my novels, I think you may find the second edition of my book *Conversations in Bloomsbury*, useful in tracing the compulsions, which led to them. For instance the three talks with T.S. Eliot and his praise of Kipling's novel *Kim*, about a pseduo orphan boy made me to write *Coolie*, about a real orphan boy.

And anti-imperialism is the cue for each novel. The '*Village Trilogy'* is in reaction to the Permanent Settlement of Lord Cornwallis.

I think it is possible for you to come to Bangalore during the forthcoming Seminar, to be held in Rangamandir, 109, J.C. Rd., Bangalore, you could have an interview with me and take down answers to the questions.

I will be staying between 23rd and 28th at the house of General Naib, 254, Defence Colony, Indra Nagar, Tel. 571610, 566185.

It is not possible to communicate to your nuances in letters.

Regards,

Lingaraja Gandhi,
No. 231, I Main,
Jayalakshmipuram,
Mysore-570012. India.

Sincerely
(Mulk Raj Anand)

LETTER—4

Mulk Raj Anand,
#25, Cuffe Parade,
Bombay-400005.
Phone Res: 2181371

6-3-96

Dear Shri Gandhi,

I apologize for not informing you about my cancelling the visit to Bangalore for Sahitya Academi Seminar.

I did not expect that old age will begin to affect my movements, as I found this happening from the daily backache, that seems to be coming on as a constant reminder that I can't even walk about as freely as I used to.

I am under good Homeopathic Doctor, but I suppose no physician can regenerate youth in an old body.

Attending the Seminar would have meant my going from a private home. I do not eat outside food and would have had to return to my abode for special diet. Besides, I need two hours sleep in the afternoon. And while all this is possible at home it would not have been possible as guest of friends, who are cordial, but have no driver to take guests about.

Please accept my apology.

And rather than take the trouble to come to Bombay, I suggest you send me a questionnaire, as also lend me the copy of the work of the other writer with whose work you are doing a comparative study.

I will try and give the answers.

The reason why your visit here may not be fruitful is because I am not certain about my programme as it is likely that I may have to go to Delhi on what dates I don't know.

Please forgive default.

Regards,

Lingaraja Gandhi,
No. 231, I Main,
Jayalakshmipuram,
Mysore-570012. India.

Sincerely
(Mulk Raj Anand)

LETTER—5

Mulk Raj Anand,
#25, Cuffe Parade,
Bombay-400005.
Phone Res: 2181371

20-8-96

Dear Shri Lingaraj Gandhi,

On my return from London, on Sunday 18th I have seen your letter of 30th July.

I went to UK for some research in British Museum, under difficult conditions, both because of age and, as it is Mrs. Thatcher's hell where every breath costs a pound!!!

Now, I will be available in Bombay on 6th, 7th September. Presumably after 4 pm.

I don't think you know, that I live in Khandala, 70 miles from Bombay, five days a week, to do my writing, and only three days in Bombay...

Can you make it on those dates, 6th and 7th.

Later, I will be going for a Seminar to Delhi, and it may be at the end of September, where I may be available.

Please bring tape recorder with you if and when you come.

I am not being precious but am strained from age and work...

Kind regards,

Lingaraja Gandhi,
No. 231, I Main,
Jayalakshmipuram,
Mysore - 570 012. India.

Sincerely
(Mulk Raj Anand)

LETTER—6

Mulk Raj Anand,
#25, Cuffe Parade,
Bombay-400005.
Phone Res: 2181371

28-9-96

Dear Shri Lingraj Gandhi,

Since you were here, I have been to Delhi to preside on a Seminar on the thesis of *Muse and the Minorities.*

It was very well attended and some highly intelligent papers were read on the writings of minority authors, as also on the theme of writers in exile, as are most of the Indian English writers.

The coincidence of the coming to be of the UF (United Front) Government of the rejected, even for a short while, made the Seminar very timely. And it is possible that we may see emergence of more Dalit writings than before.

Since you left, I have read the novel *A Grain of Wheat* by Ngugi, the Kenya novelist. It is brilliantly written, with command of English language, rare in our country. It is about the transfer of power from British to Kenya hands.

Unfortunately, this dynamic writer has chosen not to create any vital characters, but has given us the glimpses of several people from among the mass in villages of Kenya. Even Jomo Kenyatta, who was the leader of the Liberation Movement, appears in only one paragraph. And the village characters remain shadows, being un-recognizable partly because of their names. The few who are decisive are not highlighted.

Anyhow, there is no comparable novel of mine, which can be studied as a comparative creation, because I have not yet dealt with the transfer of power. Only, *Sword and the Sickle*, which is the novel of the struggle for the peasantry, may stand parallel to this liberation struggle of the folk in Kenya.

Again, I feel, that if you are doing a comparative study, of a novel by Ngugi and by myself, be careful and read *Sword and the Sickle* as a possible parallel recreation.

I hope that our conversations were fruitful.

Anyhow, please get Xeroxed copies of parts of the books, which you borrowed, but let me have, specially, book on Shakespeare back soon, by way of registered post.

With kindliest wishes,

Lingaraja Gandhi,
No. 231, I Main,
Jayalakshmipuram,
Mysore-570012. India.

Sincerely
(Mulk Raj Anand)

LETTER—7

Mulk Raj Anand,
#25, Cuffe Parade,
Bombay-400005.
Phone Res: 2181371

4th October 96.

Dear Shri Lingaraja,

I duly received the book on *Shakespeare*.

Meanwhile, I would like to repeat, what I wrote in my previous note, last week, that the only relevance of Ngugi's novel, *Grain of Wheat*, has with any novel of mine is with *Sword and the Sickle*, which is a novel of struggle, not near the time of Independence, which came fourteen years later, but in a decisive rising of the Uttar Pradesh peasantry.

In fact, I find the episodic treatment of the struggle with M.N. Roy and the Count in Kala Kankar, more pointed, and causalities seem clearer than in the rounded treatment of the narrative of Ngugi before liberation of Kenya.

Of course, there are several characters in my novel, but I think, more clearly sketched. Ngugi seems to want to indicate anonymous struggle and mentions various names, in some of their actions, without characterizing the heroes and non-heroes.

I would like your reactions to my views.

Regards,

Lingaraja Gandhi,
No. 231, I Main,
Jayalakshmipuram,
Mysore - 570 012. India.

Sincerely
(Mulk Raj Anand)

LETTER—8

Mulk Raj Anand,
#25, Cuffe Parade,
Bombay-400005.
Phone Res: 2181371

6-10-97

Dear Shri Lingaraj Gandhi,

Your letter of 26th September came to me in Khandala, where I have been recuperating from an accident in which a little chip of my right hipbone broke from a fall on slippery slope. That is why the delay in writing.

I have not yet seen the reprint of your article, which you seem to have sent me, as from the *Cross-Cultural Voices.*

The theme of the war novel, you have taken, has been rarely noticed by scholars in India, though there is a very perceptive article contributed to a Seminar in Johnstown University by an American scholar. I will send you a copy of that when I return to Bombay.

I quite understand your involvement in the thesis on Ngugi, and currently Dr. K.D. Verma, tells me he will be taking up the contrast of Kipling's *Kim* and Anand's Munoo by sometime next year. He organized a seminar of fourteen critics in Johnstown University on my writings last year.

I have noticed that only in Mysore people like Gowda, and M.K. Naik, attacked my writings for my critique of traditional taboos. In the outside world, most of the novels have been greeted with warm appreciation. The presence of *Untouchable* and *Coolie* in 'Penguin Contemporary World Classic edition' and in several reprints as also in world languages is the answer to the orthodox.

I will write to you again after I have seen your paper on *Across the Black Waters.*

Regards,

Lingaraja Gandhi,
No. 231, I Main,
Jayalakshmipuram,
Mysore-570012. India.

Sincerely
(Mulk Raj Anand)

LETTER—9

Mulk Raj Anand,
#25, Cuffe Parade,
Bombay-400005.
Phone Res: 2181371

23-10-96

Dear Friend Lingaraja,

As I am going to Delhi to receive the Veteran Writers Award from Publishers and Booksellers Association of Delhi, this letter is mere acknowledgement of your epistle than comments on your findings about Ngugi.

I find this Kenya writer's command of the English language extraordinary. Our own Indian-English writers do not seem to have such mastery, except in the case of Raja Rao, Desani and Vikram Seth.

As I myself, felt that the kinetic rhythms in all of us, which results in speech, are compulsive from early childhood, so in my opinion, being kinetic rhythms as current in natives of a languages being from early years foreigners cannot acquire the poetic currents in an alien language, though they can write prose from logic of major premise, minor premise and conclusion. That is why few Indian poets writing in English have been able to be natural and fluent in their Indian-English poetry.

In prose, feelings become thoughts and expression in an alien language is possible. Even in prose, however, the thinking is in mother tongue and the writing is in translation and adaptation in the alien language.

In Ngugi's case, there is remarkable fluency of prose, which makes me wonder whether the education system in Kenya was mostly in English language.

Of course, he succeeds in recreating a whole village as hero though characters get mixed up.

I would like to read his other novels.

But I see that, maybe from pressures of our history, our treatment of young have similarities of intent and behaviour in two different traditions of struggle for liberty. **Your thesis might reveal to both Ngugi and myself nuances, which, as authors, we have taken for granted. So I will await the completion of thesis.**

With kindliest wishes,

Lingaraja Gandhi,
No. 231, I Main, Jayalakshmipuram,
Mysore - 570 012. India.

Sincerely
(Mulk Raj Anand)

LETTER—10

Mulk Raj Anand,
#25, Cuffe Parade,
Bombay-400005.
Phone Res: 2181371

1-1-97

Dear Shri Lingraj,

Not because it is conventional but really because I wish young colleagues like you to flourish, I hope this year will extend your consciousness beyond your researches into areas of what is Literature?

I feel, after having been to Pattan to inaugurate a seminar on Indian English Writings that both teachers and taught have, unfortunately, been deprived of awareness of world literature or rather the classics, which makes their learning's in the universities half-baked. Mysore University is an exception. Maybe because Prof. C.D. Narasimhaiah went to Cambridge and studied under Leavis. He lectured on his tutor. Unfortunately he did not mention Queenie Leavis, hostess and scholar equal to her husband, who made tea for guest students, but also participated in discussions, often expressing opinions against her husband's views.

The purpose of this note is to apologize for not answering your questionnaire.

Instead, I am asking for a favour.

As University of Kurukshetra in Haryana has offerred *Coolie* as extra book for B.A. Hons. degree, Mssrs Frank Bros. of New Delhi, wish to issue a text book edition of this novel, in the same style as Geetha Book House published *Untouchable*, which went into three large editions.

In the Geetha Book House edition, I added an appendix on the genesis of *Untouchable* and CDN got me a long note written by Dr. Damodar Rao, as an 'afterword.'

I have felt that he might write a similar note for *Coolie* to go as an appendix. Now, Dr. Damodar Rao, I understand, is not well.

I wonder if you could consider adding an afterword of two to three thousand words, to meet the student's need to explication of the inspiration from which *Coolie* was written. From within hill village of Shimla to see the wonders of the world, of the child-hero-anti-hero, who goes to a small town, big city, and ends up in the mountains to die as a 'Rickshaw coolie,' is symbolic of millions of young boys, who have to leave village homes to earn a living in a world which they think is paradise but turns out to be hell.

I wrote my novel against Eliot's admiration for the pseduo orphan boy hero KIM, which the poet liked.

I went to my room after he said this and began to write *Coolie* about the real orphan boy as against Kipling's pseduo half-caste hero, who fells a pathan, six foot high, turns secret agent and is supposed to be an empire-builder.

My novel went into three impressions in a week after publication. It is a 'world book' in twenty-eight languages, sold half a million copies in Russia, but has been called communist propaganda by some of our intelligentsia.

If you will agree to do an essay of two to three thousand words or so, I will see that you are paid for your work.

I will send you rare reviews by Prichertt, Bowra, and Narasimhaiah himself, which may give you some idea of the warm reception this novel got after seventeen rejections of *Untouchable.*

I do hope you can do this favour, so that students, who are usually naive, may get to know how this novel has been called the equal of *Uncle Tom's Cabin.* Except that it has not yet liberated thirty million young boys working in Carpet factories and Bidi making shops!

I also want this novel to be translated into Kannada. Who will undertake that?

I am asking Geetha Book House.

With kind regards,

Lingaraja Gandhi,
No. 231, I Main,
Jayalakshmipuram,
Mysore-570012. India.

Sincerely
(Mulk Raj Anand)

LETTER—11

Mulk Raj Anand,
#25, Cuffe Parade,
Bombay-400005.
Phone Res: 2181371

25-1-97

Dear Shri Lingraj Gandhi

I have not been upto much work in the severe cold of last week, but I did receive your reassuring letter: that you will do a note of about 2000 to 1500 words for text book edition of *Coolie* to go as an appendix for students like the note by Dr. Damodar Rao, which was included as an 'afterword' in my Geetha Book House edition of *Untouchable*.

I have taken your suggestion of possible translation of *Coolie* into Kannada language by Dr. Ramachandra. I have written to him a letter of which I enclose a copy.

In spite of everything, I do my 'tapasya' on the Gandhian Saga.

I wish, however, at this stage, that the early novels go into a collected works edition.

With warm regards,

Lingaraja Gandhi,
No. 231, I Main,
Jayalakshmipuram,
Mysore-570012. India.

Sincerely
(Mulk Raj Anand)

LETTER—12

Mulk Raj Anand,
#25, Cuffe Parade,
Bombay-400005.
Phone Res: 2181371

31-1-97

Dear Friend, Shri Lingraj,

This is about the afterword of Coolie!

I understand from Dr. George John from Jodhpur University, who initiated the idea of the textbook edition of *Coolie* that the Publisher in Delhi answers demand of Universities in North India, by only issuing abridged editions of novels.

But, never will I allow an abridged edition of any of my novels, to be published.

One inadequate rendering of *Coolie* was done by a lady and published by Arnold without my permission.

I feel, that this is the kind of thing that makes for third-rate students in our Universities. Surely, if a student for B.A. degree cannot read a novel in original form, and can only accept abridged edition, then standards become so low as to make the graduates inferior even to London Metric, where a full novel of Dickens, Thackray or Hardy is offerred.

So please don't trouble about the afterword. But you can contrast *Coolie* and *Kim* one day: The real orphan boy against the fantasy orphan hero of Kipling, whom T.S. Eliot admired.

No hurry about this, but it is a very possible theme when you have time.

Warm regards,

Lingaraja Gandhi,
No. 231, I Main,
Jayalakshmipuram,
Mysore-570012. India.

Sincerely
(Mulk Raj Anand)

LETTER—13

Mulk Raj Anand,
#25, Cuffe Parade,
Bombay-400005.
Phone Res: 2181371

16th April, 1997

Dear Shri Lingaraja Gandhi,

As you know, I spend four days in our Khandala Sarvodhya Sabha and three days in Mumbai, so, the delay in acknowledgement of your letter of 4th April.

Synopsis of your thesis shows acute perceptiveness of motive forces behind my novels and Ngugi wa Thiong'o, Kenya.

As you have not been constrained by Indian Academicians to see political implications in both these novelists, your thesis will be valuable for the new young students.

Somewhere in your thesis you might refer to my talks with T.S. Eliot during which I dared to put our anti-colonial attitude.

Actually, I wrote *Coolie* in reaction against Eliot's praise of Kipling's *Kim*. He said, that Kipling's *Kim* is exemplary novel of India. I went up in a huff to begin writing about a real orphan boy Munoo, as against pseudo orphan hero of Kipling, who falls a strong pattan and does espionage work for the Empire.

Anyhow, it is time that some of our young wrote a parallel to Edward Said's *Orientalism* and *Culture and Imperialism*.

Regards,

Lingaraja Gandhi,
No. 231, I Main,
Jayalakshmipuram,
Mysore - 570 012. India.

Sincerely
(Mulk Raj Anand)

LETTER—14

Mulk Raj Anand,
#25, Cuffe Parade,
Bombay-400005.
Phone Res: 2181371

30th April, 1997

Dear Shri Lingaraja Gandhi,

I did write to you my appreciation of your synopsis of thesis.

Your degree is assured...

If and when you are in position to advise Board of Studies, you might consider suggesting to Members that they adopt both these novels as Extra Texts for B.A. degree.

Warm regards,
Lingaraja Gandhi,
No. 231, I Main,
Jayalakshmipuram,
Mysore-570012. India.

Sincerely
(Mulk Raj Anand)

LETTER—15

Mulk Raj Anand,
#25, Cuffe Parade,
Bombay-400005.
Phone Res: 2181371

30th May, 1997

Dear Lingraj:

Do go ahead with essay on *Kim* and *Coolie*! It is an important theme to show my beginnings of Imperialist projections.

More later.

Warm regards
Lingaraja Gandhi,
No. 231, I Main,
Jayalakshmipuram,
Mysore-570012. India.

Sincerely
(Mulk Raj Anand)

A Selected Bibliography

WORKS BY MULK RAJ ANAND

Fiction

Anand, Mulk Raj. *Untouchable.* 1935. New Delhi: Arnold Publishers, 1981.

——. *Coolie.* 1936. New Delhi: Arnold Publishers, 1981.

——. *Two Leaves and a Bud.* 1937. New Delhi: Arnold Associates, 1994.

——. *Lament on the Death of a Master of Arts.* Lucknow: Naya Sansar, 1938.

——. *The Village.* 1939. New Delhi: Arnold Publishers, 1984.

——. *Across the Black Waters.* 1940. New Delhi: Orient Paperbacks, 1980.

——. *The Sword and the Sickle.* 1942. New Delhi: Arnold Publishers, 1984.

——. *The Big Heart.* 1945. New Delhi: Arnold-Heinemann, 1980.

——. *Private Life of an Indian Prince.* 1953. New Delhi: Arnold Publishers, 1984.

——. *The Old Woman and the Cow.* 1960. Rpt. as Gauri. New Delhi: Arnold Publishers, 1981.

——. *The Road.* 1961. New Delhi: Sterling Publishers, 1987.

——. *Death of a Hero.* 1961. New Delhi: Arnold Publishers, 1985.

Autobiographical Novels

Anand, Mulk Raj. *Seven Summers.* 1951. New Delhi: Arnold Publishers, 1986.

Anand, Mulk Raj. *Morning Face.* (Bombay: Kutub-Popular), 1968. New Delhi: Arnold Publishers, 1976.

——. *Confession of a Lover.* New Delhi: Arnold Publishers, 1984.

——. *The Bubble.* New Delhi: Arnold Publishers, 1990.

——. *Pilpali Sahab.* New Delhi: Arnold Publishers, 1990.

——. *Little Plays of Mahatma Gandhi.* New Delhi: Arnold Publishers, 1991.

——. *Caliban and Gandhi.* New Delhi: Arnold Publishers, 1992.

Short Stories

Anand, Mulk Raj. *The Lost Child and Other Stories.* London: J.A. Allen, 1934.

——. *The Barber's Trade Union and Other Stories.* 1944. New Delhi: Arnold Publishers, 1984.

——. *The Tractor and the Corn Goddess and Other Stories.* 1947. New Delhi: Arnold Publishers, 1987.

——. *Reflection on the Golden Bed and Other Stories.* 1954. New Delhi: Arnold Publishers, 1988.

——. *Selected Stories.* 1954. New Delhi: Arnold Publishers, 1987.

——. *The Power of Darkness and Other Stories.* Bombay: Jaico Publishing House, 1959.

——. *Lajwanti and Other Stories.* Bombay: Jaico Publishing House, 1966.

——. *Between Tears and Laughter.* New Delhi: Sterling Publishers, 1973.

Non-Fiction

Anand, Mulk Raj. *The Golden Breath: Studies in Five Poets of the New India.* London: John Murray, 1933.

——. "Mr. Eliot's Kipling." *Life and Letters Today.* 32.55 (1942).

——. "The Place of India." *Writers in Freedom.* Ed. Herman Ould. London: Lindsay Drummond, 1943.

Anand, Mulk Raj. "I Believe in Man." *In Search of Faith.* Ed. Ernest W. Martin. London: Lindsay Drummond, 1943.

——. Preface. *The Novel and the People.* By Ralph Fox. London: Cobbett Publishing, 1944.

——. "Rabindranath Tagore." *New Spirit.* Ed. J.W.L. Martin. London: Dennis Dobson, 1946.

——. *Apology for Heroism: An Essay in Search of Faith.* 1946. Bombay: Kutub-Popular, 1957.

——. *Homage to Tagore.* Lahore: Sangam Publishers, 1946.

——. *The King Emperor's English.* Bombay: Hindi Kitabs, 1948.

——. *Lines Written to an Indian Air.* Bombay: Nalanda Publishers, 1949.

——. *The Story of Man.* Amritsar: Sikh Publishing House, 1952.

——. *The Story of India.* Bombay: Kutub-Popular, 1954.

——. "Trends in the Novel." *Cultural Forum.* (Nov. 1961).

——. "New Bearings in Indian Literature." *The Literary Review.* 4.4 (1961).

——. *Is There a Contemporary Indian Civilization?* Bombay: Asia Publishing House, 1963.

——. "Letter to E.M. Forster." *E.M. Forster: A Tribute.* Ed. K. Natwar Singh, New York: Harcourt, 1964.

——. "East West Dialogue." *Indian Writers in Conference.* Ed. Nissim Ezekiel. Bombay: P.E.N. All India Centre, 1964.

——. "A Note on Modern Indian Fiction." *Indian Literature.* 8.1 (1965).

——. "Is Universal Criticism Possible?" *Literary Criticism: European and Indian Traditions.* Ed. C.D. Narasimhaiah. Mysore: University of Mysore, 1966.

——. "Requiem for Mr. Eliot." *T.S. Eliot: Homage from India.* Ed. P. Lal. Calcutta: Writers Workshop, 1965.

——. "The Role of Creative Writers and Artists in the Developing Countries of Afro-Asia." *Afro-Asia and World Affairs.* 3.1 (1966).

Anand, Mulk Raj. "The Sources of Creative Writing." *Indian Literature.* 7 (Sept. 1967).

——. "The Story of My Experiment with a White Lie." Indian Literature. 10.3 (1967). Rpt. in *Critical Essays on Indian Writing in English.* Ed. M.K. Naik *et al.* 1968. Madras: Macmillan, 1977.

——. "Conversation with Mahatma Gandhi." *Mahatma Gandhi: One Hundred Years.* Ed. S. Radhakrishnan. New Delhi: Gandhi Peace Foundation, 1968.

——. "The Question of Modernity." *Modernity and Contemporary Indian Literature.* Simla: Indian Institute of Advanced Studies, 1968.

——. "I Believe..." *The Illustrated Weekly of India.* 90.43 (1969). Rpt in *I Believe.* Ed. Khushwant Singh. New Delhi: Hindi Pocket Books, n.d.

——. "Profile of E.M. Forster." *The Literary Half-Yearly.* 10.2 (1969).

——. "Old Myths and New Myths: Recital Versus Novel." The Banasthali Patrika. 5.13 (1969). Rpt. in *Indian Literature of the Past Fifty Years.* Ed. C.D. Narasimhaiah. Mysore: University of Mysore, 1970.

——. "What Good is Literature For?" *The Banasthali Patrika.* 5.14 (1970).

——. "About the Lost Child and Other Allegories." *Indian Literature.* 13.1 (1970).

——. *The Humanism of M.K. Gandhi.* Chandigarh: University of Chandigarh 1971.

——. "Pigeon-Indian: Some Notes of Indian English Writing." *Studies in Australian and Indian Literature: Proceedings of a Seminar.* Ed. C.D. Narasimhaiah and S. Nagarajan. New Delhi, 1971.

——. *Roots and Flowers: Two Lectures on the Metamorphosis of Technique and Content in the Indian Novel.* Dharwar: Karnataka University, 1972.

——. "The Changeling—An Indo-Anglian Novelist's Credo." *Indian and Foreign Review.* 9.23 (1972).

Anand, Mulk Raj. "Trends in the Modern Indian Novel." *The Journal of Indian Writing in English.* 1.1 (1973).

——. "The Changeling." *World Literature Written in English.* 15.1 (1976).

——. "Why I Write?" *Indo-English Literature: A Collection of Critical Essays.* Ed. K.K. Sharma. Ghaziabad: Vimal Prakashan, 1977. Rpt. in *Kakatiya Journal of English Studies.* 2.1 (1977) and *Perspectives on Mulk Raj Anand.* Ed. K.K. Sharma. Ghaziabad: Vimal Prakashan, 1978, and *Indian Writing in English.* Ed. Krishna Nandan Sinha, New Delhi: Heritage Publishers, 1979.

——. "On the Use of Epithets, Swear Words and Abuses." *Littcrit.* 2.4 (1977).

——. "An Undeclared War: The Internecine War between Brown Sahibs and Bahus." *Littcrit.* 3.1 (1978): 11-24.

——. "Content and Form in *Untouchable* and *Kanthapura.*" *Littcrit.* 14 (June 1982).

——. "Reflections of a Novelist: Some Notes on the Novel." *Indian Readings in Commonwealth Literature.* Ed. G.S. Amur *et al.* New Delhi: Sterling Publishers, 1985.

——. "New Year's Thoughts 1-1-1986," "The Sources of Protest in My Novels." *Contemporary Indian Fiction in English.* Ed. K. Ayyappa Paniker. Trivandrum: Institute of English, University of Kerala, n.d.

——. "On Power and Violence." *The Hindu.* January 17, 1993.

——. "The Nehruvian Legacy." *The Hindu.* May 9, 1993.

——. "The March of the Indian Novel." *The Hindu.* May 1, 1994.

——. "Importance of English." *The Hindu.* June 19, 1994.

WORKS BY NGUGI WA THIONG'O

Fiction

Thiong'o, Ngugi wa. *Weep Not, Child.* 1964. London: Heinemann, 1985.

Thiong'o, Ngugi wa. *The River Between.* 1965. London: Heinemann, 1988.

——. *A Grain of Wheat.* 1967. London: Heinemann, 1988.

——. *Petals of Blood.* 1977. London: Heinemann, 1987.

——. *Devil On the Cross.* 1982. Trans. Ngugi wa Thiong'o. London: Heinemann, 1987.

——. *Matigari.* 1987. Trans. Wangui wa Goro. London: Heinemann, 1989.

Short Story

Thiong'o, Ngugi wa. *Secret Lives.* 1975. London: Heinemann, 1986.

Non-Fiction

Thiong'o, Ngugi wa. *Homecoming: Essays on African and Caribbean Literature, Culture and Politics.* 1972. London: Heinemann, 1982.

——. *The Writers in Politics.* London: Heinemann, 1981.

——. *Detained: A Writer's Prison Diary.* 1981. London: Heinemann, 1984.

——. *Barrel of a Pen: Resistance to Repression in Neo-Colonial Kenya.* Trenton N.J.: Africa World Press, 1985.

——. *Decolonizing the Mind: The Politics of Language in African Literature.* 1986. London: James Currey, 1987.

——. *Moving the Centre: The Struggle for Cultural Freedoms.* London: James Currey, 1993.

——. Introduction. *Africa's Cultural Revolution.* By Okot p' Betek. Nairobi: Macmillan, 1973.

——. "Education For a National Culture" *UFAHAMU.* 12.2 (1982). 20-34.

——. "On Writing in Gikuyu." Research in African Literatures. 16.2 (1985). 151-55.

——. "Decolonizing the Means of Imagination." *Symphony of Freedom.* Ed. Varavara Rao. Hyderabad, India: All India Peoples Resistance Forum, (1996). 281-87.

WORKS ON MULK RAJ ANAND

Agnihotri G.N. "Mulk Raj Anand—His Progressive Proletarianism." *Indian Life and Problems in the Novels of Mulk Raj Anand, Raja Rao and R.K. Narayan.* Meerut: Shalabh Prakashan, 1993. 28-60.

Amur, G.S. *Forbidden Fruit: Essays on Indo-Anglian Fiction.* Calcutta: Writers Workshop, 1992.

Asnani, Shyam M. "Social Protest in Mulk Raj Anand." *Critical Response To Indian English Fiction.* Delhi: Mittal Publications, 1985. 10-24.

——. "A Critique of Mulk Raj Anand's Literary Creed." *New Dimensions of Indian English Novel.* Delhi: Doaba House, 1987. 116-31.

Badal, R.K. "Mulk Raj Anand." *Indo-Anglian Literature: An Outline.* Badal, R.K. Bareily: Prakash Book Depot, 1975. 29-38.

Bald, Suresh Renjen. *Novelists and Political Consciousness.* Delhi: Chanakya Publications, 1982.

——. "Politics of a Revolutionary Elite: A Study of Mulk Raj Anand's Novels." *Modern Asian Studies,* 8.4 (1974).

Berry, Margaret. *Mulk Raj Anand: The Man and the Novelist.* Amsterdam: Oriental Press, 1971.

Bhatnagar, K.C. *Realism in Major Indo-English Fiction.* Bareilly: Prakash Book Depot, 1980.

Bhattacharya, B.K. "Two Leaves and a Bud: Truth and Fiction." *Kakatiya Journal of English Studies.* 2.1 (1977).

Calder-Marshal. Rev. of *Across the Black Waters. Life and Letters Today.* 28.4 (1941).

Chandra, Suresh. *Culture and Criticism.* Delhi: B.R. Publishing Corporation, 1987.

Chellappan, K. "The Child Archetype in the Commonwealth Short Stories: Katherine Mansfield, Janet Frame and Mulk Raj Anand." *Recent Commonwealth Literature.* 1. Ed. R.K. Dhavan *et al.* New Delhi: Prestige Books, 1969.

Cowasjee, Saros. *Coolie: An Assessment.* Delhi: Oxford University Press, 1976.

——. "Mulk Raj Anand: Princess and Proletarians." *The Journal of Commonwealth Literature* (July, 1968).

——. *So Many Freedoms: A Study of The Major Fiction of Mulk Raj Anand.* Delhi: Oxford University Press, 1977.

——. "Mulk Raj Anand: The Fusion of History and Fiction." *Subjects Worthy Fame,* Ed. A.L. Macleod. New Delhi: Sterling Publishers, 1989. 17-26.

Cowasjee, Saros.*Studies in Indian and Anglo-Indian Fiction.* New Delhi: Indus-Harper Colins, 1993.

Desai, S.K. "The Theme of Childhood in Commonwealth Fiction." *Commonwealth Literature: Problems of Response.* Ed. C.D. Narasimhaiah. Madras: Macmillan, 1981. 25-37.

Dhawan, R.K. Ed. *The Novels of Mulk Raj Anand.* New Delhi: Prestige Books, 1992.

Dobree, Bonamy. Rev. of *Across the Black Waters. The Spectator.* 5865, 2 Nov. 1940.

Dommergues, Andre. "An Interpretation of Anand's *Untouchable.*" *Commonwealth.* 8.1 (1985): 14-23.

Dwivedi, S.C. "Existentialism in Anand's *Across the Black Waters.*" *Indian Fiction in English: Problems and Promises.* Pathak, R.S. Ed. New Delhi: Northern Book Centre, 1990.

Figuria, Dorothy. "Mulk Raj Anand: Europe as an Object of Orientalist Discourse." *South Asian Review,* 15.12 (1991).

Fisher, Marlene. *The Wisdom of the Heart: A Study of the Works of Mulk Raj Anand.* New Delhi: Sterling Publishers, 1985.

——. "Interview with Mulk Raj Anand: May 19, 1973, Khandala." *World Literature Written in English,* 13.1 (1974).

——. "Mulk Raj Anand's Confessional Novels." *Journal of Indian Writing in English.* 4.2 (1976).

——. "Mulk Raj Anand as Autobiographer." *New Perspectives*

in Indian Literature in English: Essays in Honour of Professor M.K. Naik. Ed. Yaravantitemath et al. New Delhi: Sterling Publishers, 1955. 177-85.

Forster, E.M. Preface. *Untouchable*. New Delhi: Arnold Associates, 1981.

Gandhi, Lingaraja. "Excursion to Continental Graveyard: A Reading of Anand's *Across the Black Waters*." *Cross Cultural Voices*. Ed. Claudio Garlier and Isabella Maria Zoppi, Roma: Bulzoni, 1997.

Gandhi, Lingaraja. "Mulk Raj Anand: Quest For So Many Freedoms": Bangalore: *Sunday Herald*, October 3, 2004.

George, C.J. *Mulk Raj Anand: His Art and Concern* (A Study of His Non-Autobiographical Novels). New Delhi: Atlantic Publishers, 1994.

Gowda, H.H. Anniah. "Mulk Raj Anand." *The Literary Half-Yearly*, 6.1 (1968).

Goyal, Bhagavat S. "Mulk Raj Anand—The Writer as Humanist." *Culture and Commitment: Aspects of Indian Literature in English*. Goyal Bhagavat S. Meerut: Shalabh Book House, 1984.

Gupta, G.S. Balarama. "Mulk Raj Anand's *Untouchable*: The Dialectics of Self-Affirmation." *Perspectives on Indian Fiction in English*. Ed. Naik, M.K. New Delhi: Abhinav Publications, 1985. 13-20.

——. *Mulk Raj Anand: A Study of His Fiction in Humanist Perspective*. Bareilly: Prakash Book Depot, 1974.

Gupta, Sangeeta. "The Nature of Brother-Sister Relationship: Untouchable, *A Bend in the Ganges*, and *A Situation in New Delhi*." *Recent Commonwealth Literature*. 1 Ed. R.K. Dhawan *et al.* New Delhi: Prestige Books, 1989.

——. "Towards a Closer Understanding of Anand." *Perspectives on Mulk Raj Anand*. Ed. K.K. Sharma. Ghaziabad: Vimal Prakashan, 1978. 9-15.

Harrex, S.C. *The Fire and the Offering: The English Language Novel of India 1935-70*. Vol. 1. Calcutta: A Writers Workshop Publications, 1977.

Harrex, S.C. "Western Ideology and Eastern Form of Fiction: The Case of Mulk Raj Anand." *Asian and Western Writers in Dialogue: New Cultural Identities.* Ed. Guy Amirthanayagam. London: Macmillan, 1982.

Hemenway, Stephen Ignatius. "Pioneers of the Indo-Anglian Novel: Mulk Raj Anand." *The Novel of India.* Vol. 2. Hemenway Stephen Ignatius. Calcutta: Writers Workshop Publications, 1975.

Iyengar, K.R. Srinivasa. *Indian Writing in English.* 1962. New Delhi: Sterling Publishers, 1995.

Jain, Jasbir. "Gandhi and the Indian Novel in English." *Problems of Postcolonial Literatures and Other Essays.* By Jain. Jaipur: Printwell Publishers, 1991. 83-85.

Jhan, Rama. *Gandhian Thought and Indo-Anglian Novelists.* Delhi: Chanakya Publications, 1983.

Kalinnikova, Elina J. *Indian-English Literature: A Perspective.* Trans. Pal Sharma. Ed. K.K. Sharma. Ghaziabad: Vimal Prakashan, 1982.

Karnani, Chetan. *Indian Writing in English.* New Delhi: Arnold Associates, 1995.

Kohil Suresh. "I don't believe in Indian Critics: An Interview with Anand." *The Hindu,* Dec. 19, 1993.

——. *Mulk Raj Anand: A Critical Essay.* Bombay: Hind-Kutub, 1948.

Lindsay, Jack. *The Elephant and the Lotus: A Study of the Novels of Mulk Raj Anand.* Bombay: Popular-Kutub, 1965.

Mehta, P.P. "Mulk Raj Anand—The Novelist of the Underdog." *Indo-Anglian Fiction: An Assessment.* Mehta P.P. Bareilly: Prakash Book Depot, 1979. 148-96.

Mukherjee, Arun P. "The Exclusions of Postcolonial Theory and Mulk Raj Anand's *Untouchable*: A Case Study." Ariel, 22:3, 1991.

Mukherjee, Meenakshi. "Beyond the Village: An Aspect of Mulk Raj Anand." *Critical Essays on Indian Writing in*

English. Ed. M.K. Naik *et al.* 1968. Madras: Macmillan, 1977.

Murti, K.V. Suryanarayana. *The Sword and the Sickle: A Study of Mulk Raj Anand's Novel.* Mysore: Geetha Book House, 1982.

Naik, M.K. Ed. "The Achievement of Mulk Raj Anand." *Mulk Raj Anand.* New Delhi: Arnold-Heinemann India, 1973. 174-86.

—— Ed. *Perspectives on Indian Fiction in English.* New Delhi: Abhinav Publications, 1985.

Narasimhaiah, C.D. "Mulk Raj Anand—The Novel of Human Centrality." *The Swan and the Eagle.* 1968. Simla: Indian Institute of Advanced Study, 1987.

Niven, Alastair. *The Yoke of Pity: A Study in the Fictional Writings of Mulk Raj Anand.* New Delhi: Arnold-Heinemann, 1978.

Pacham, Gillian. "Mulk Raj Anand and the Thirties Movement in England." *Perspectives on Mulk Raj Anand.* Ed. K.K. Sharma. Ghaziabad: Vimal Prakashan, 1978. 52-63.

Paniker, K. Ayyappa. Ed. *Contemporary Indian Fiction in English.* Trivandrum: University of Kerala, 1988.

Parry, Graham. "Anand, Orwell and the War." *Explorations in Modern Indian-English Fiction.* Ed. R.K. Dhawan. New Delhi: Bahri Publications, 1982. 80-89.

Pathak, R.S. Ed. *Indian Fiction in English: Problems and Promises.* New Delhi: Sterling Publishers, 1983.

Paul, Premila. *The Novels of Mulk Raj Anand: A Thematic Study*: New Delhi: Sterling Publishers, 1983.

Pontes, Hilda. "Anand's *Untouchable*: A Classic Experimentation of Theme and Technique." *Studies in Indian Fiction in English.* Ed. G.S. Balarama Gupta. Gulbarga: JIWE, 1987. 128-41.

Rajan, P.K. *Studies in Mulk Raj Anand.* New Delhi: Abhinav Publications, 1986.

——. *Mulk Raj Anand: A Revaluation.* New Delhi: Arnold Associates, 1995.

Ram, Atma. "Mulk Raj Anand: The Novelist of Protest." *Indian Poetry and Fiction in English.* New Delhi: Bahri Publications, 1991. 15-21.

Ramamurthy, S. *The Novels of Charles Dickens and Mulk Raj Anand: A Comparative Study.* Tiruchi: S. Ramamurthy, 1994.

Rao, Damodar. "Social and Political Awareness in the Novels of Mulk Raj Anand and George Orwell" Diss. Mysore University, 1979.

——. Afterword. Untouchable. 1935. Mysore: Geetha Book House, 1992.

Reddy, K. Venkata. "Cruelty of Man to Man: *Two Leaves and a Bud.*" *Major Indian Novelists.* New Delhi: Prestige Books, 1990. 16-24.

Rickword, Edgell. "Three Views on Coolie." *The Novels of Mulk Raj Anand.* Ed. R.K. Dhawan. Prestige Books, 1992. 78-83.

Riemeinschneider, Dieter. *An Ideal of Man in Mulk Raj Anand's Novels.* Bombay: Popular-Kutub, 1967.

Robertson, R.T. "*Untouchable* as an Archetypal Novel." *The Novels of Mulk Raj Anand.* Ed. R.K. Dhawan. New Delhi: Prestige Books, 1992. 98-104.

Sharma, Ambuj Kumar. *The Theme of Exploitation in the Novels of Mulk Raj Anand.* New Delhi: H.K. Publishers, 1990.

Sharma, K.K. Ed. *Perspectives on Mulk Raj Anand.* Ghaziabad: Vimal Prakashan, 1978.

Shivapuri, Jagadish. "Mulk Raj Anand's *The Road*: An Interpretation." Littcrit 22 & 23 (1986): 19-26.

Sinha, Krishna Nandan. "The Mythical Parallel: A Study in Anand's Later Fiction." *Response: Recent Revelations of Indian Fiction in English.* Ed. Prasad Hari Mohan. Bareily: Prakash Book Depot, 1983.

Varghese, Paul C. "The Proletarian Humanism of Mulk Raj Anand." *Problems of the Indian Creative Writer in English.* Bombay: Somaiya Publications, 1971.

Verma, K.D. "Ideological Confrontation and Synthesis in Mulk Raj Anand's *Conversations in Bloomsbury.*" *Journal of South-Asian Literature.* 28. 1802 (1994).

——. "Understanding Mulk Raj Anand: An Introduction." *South-Asian Review.* (The Mulk Raj Anand. Special Number). 15.12 (1991).

Walsh, William. "Fiction: The Founding Fathers—Mulk Raj Anand, Raja Rao and R.K. Narayan." *Indian Literature in English.* Ed. Carroll David and Michael Wheeler, USA: Longman, 1990. 62-97.

Williams, Haydn Moore. "Mulk Raj Anand: Realism and Politics." *Studies in Modern Indian Fiction in English.* Vol. 1. Calcutta: A Writers Workshop Publishers, 1973.

Special Issue

South Asian Review. 15.12 (1991).

WORKS ON NGUGI WA THIONG'O

Aborisade P.A. "National and Revolutionary Consciousness: Two Phases of Ngugi's Praxis." *UFAHAMU.* 18.2 (1980). 59-74.

Acworth, William. "Interview with Ngugi wa Thiong'o." *UFAHAMU.* 18.2 (1990). 41-46.

Adecko, Adeleke. Story-Telling As Dialectics: The Example of *Petals of Blood.*" Commonwealth Fiction. Singapore: ACLALS Bulletin. 1986.

Afejuku, Tony. "Autobiography As History and Political Treatment." *World Literature Written in English.* 30.1 (1990) 78-87.

Ahmed, Kabir. "Oral Tradition As an Instrument of Revolutionary Change in Ngugi wa Thiong'o's *Devil on the Cross.*" *UFAHAMU.* 20.2 (1992): 18-32.

Amuta, Chidi. "The Revolutionary Imperatives in the Contemporary Novel: Ngugi's *Petals of Blood* and Armah's *The Healers.*" *Commonwealth Novel in English.* 3.2 (1990): 130-142.

Anna Rutherford *et al.* "Interview with Ngugi wa Thiong'o." *Kunapipi.* 3.2 (1981): 135-140.

Balogun, Odun F. "Ngugi's *Petals of Blood.*" *Bashiru.* 10.2 (1981): 49-57.

Bamiro, Edmund O. "Recasting the Centre: Ngugi wa Thiong'o and the Africanization of English." *Kunapipi.* 16.2 (1994).

Boehmer, Elleke. "The Master's Dance to the Master's Voice: Revolutionary Nationalism and the Representation of Women in the Writing of Ngugi wa Thiong'o." *Journal of Commonwealth Literature.* 26.1 (1991)188-197.

Berger, Roger A. "Ngugi's Comic Vision." *Research in African Literature.* 20.1 (1989) 1-25.

Bjorkman, Ingrid. "Interview with Ngugi wa Thiong'o." *Kunapipi.* 40.2 (1982) 127-134.

Cook, David. "A New Birth: A Study of Ngugi wa Thiong'o *A Grain of Wheat.*" *African Literature Today.* 7 (1975).

Cook, David and Michael Okenimpke. *Ngugi wa Thiong'o: An Exploration of His Writings.* London: Heinemann, 1983.

Crehan, Stewart. "The Politics of the Signifier: Ngugi wa Thiong'o's *Petals of Blood.*" *World Literature Written in English.* 26.1 (1982) 1-24.

Dhar, T.N. "The Complete Web of the Colonial Encounter in Ngugi's Fiction." *Colonial Consciousness in Black American, African and Indian Fiction in English.* Ed. Ramesh K. Srivastava, Jalandhar, India: ABS Publications, 1991. 60-69.

Duerden, D. and Pieterse C. Eds. *African Writers Talking.* London: Heinemann, 1972.

Elders, Derek. "*A Grain of Wheat*: A Review." *African Literature Today.* 1 (1968) 1-54.

Eyoh, Hansel Nodumbe. "Interview with Ngugi wa Thiong'o." *Journal of Commonwealth Literature.* 21 (1986) 162-66.

——. "Language As Carrier of Peoples' Culture: An Interview with Ngugi wa Thiong'o." *UFAHAMU.* 14.3 (1985).

Gikandi, Simon. "Ngugi's Conversion: Writing and the Politics of Language". *Research in African Literatures.* 23.1 (1992).

——. "Community, Character and Consciousness in Sembene Ousmane's *God's Bits of Wood,* Alex La Guma's *In the Fog of the Season's End* and Ngugi's *Petals of Blood.*" *Reading the African Novel.* 1987. Nairobi: James Currey and Heinemann, 1992.

Glinga, Werner. "*The River Between* and Its Forerunners—A Contribution to the Theory of the Kenyan Novel." *World Literature Written in English.* 26.2 (1986) 211-228.

Goodwin K.L. "Nationality Chauvinism Must Burn Utopian Visions in *Petals of Blood* and *Matigari.*" *The Literary Criterion.* 26.3 (1991) 1-14.

Gowda, H.H.A. "Ngugi wa Thiong'o As Novelist." *The Literary Half-Yearly.* 16.2 (1975) 27-51.

Ikiddeh, Ime. "James Ngugi As a Novelist." *African Literature Today.* 1-4 (1969) 30-10.

——. "Ngugi wa Thiong'o: The Novelist As Historian." *A Celebration of Black African Writing.* Ed. Bruce King and Kolawole Ogungbeson. London: Oxford University Press, (1975). 204-16.

Jabbi, Bu. Buakei. "Conrad's Influence On Betrayal in *A Grain of Wheat.*" *Research in African Literatures.* 2.1 (1980) 50-83.

Jussawalla, Feroza and Reed Way Dasenbrock. "Ngugi wa Thiong'o." Interviews with Writers of the Post-Colonial World. Jacksons, London: University Press of Mississippi, (1992). 25-41.

Johnson, Joyce. "A Note on 'Theng'eta' in Ngugi wa Thiong'o's *Petals of Blood.*" *World Literature Written in English.* 28.1 (1988) 12-15.

Kamenju, Grant. "*Petals of Blood* as a Mirror of the African Revolution." *Marxism and African Literature.* Ed. George M. Gugelberger. Trenton: Africa World Press, 1985.

Ker, David I. "The Multiple Perspective I: Joseph Conrad, Nostromo; Ngugi wa Thiong'o, *Petals of Blood.*" *The*

African Novel and the Modernist Tradition. New York: Peter Lang, (1997). 75-102.

Killam, G.D. *An Introduction to the Writings of Ngugi wa Thiong'o.* London Heinemann, 1980.

——. "Literature and Society in Colonial and Post-Colonial Society in Kenya—Ngugi and Education." *The Colonial and Neo-Colonial Encounters in Commonwealth Literature.* Ed. H.H. Anniah Gowda. Mysore. Prasaranga, 1983.

Lindfors, Bernth. "Ngugi wa Thiong'o's Early Journalism." *World Literature Written in English.* 20.1-2 23-41.

Magine, Magina. "Interview with Ngugi wa Thiong'o." *African Report.* 90 (1979). 30-31.

Mamudu, Ayo. "Tracing a Winding Stair: Ngugi's Negative Methods in *Petals of Blood.*" *World Literature Written in English.* 28.1 (1988). 16-25.

Martini, Jurgen. "Ngugi wa Thiong'o: East African Novelist." *Individual and Community in Commonwealth Literature.* Ed. Daniel Massa. Malta: University Press, 1979.

Martini, Jurgen et al. "Interview with Ngugi wa Thiong'o." *Kunapipi.* 3.1 (1981) 110+.

Maughan-Brown, David. *Land, Freedom and Fiction: History and Ideology in Kenya.* London: Zed Books, 1985.

——. "Four Sons of One Father: A Comparative of Ngugi's Earliest Novels with Works by Mwangi Mangua and Wachira." *Research in African Literatures.* 16 (1985) 179-209.

Mazuri, Alamin and Lupenga Mphande. "The Historical Imperative in African Literature." *UFAHAMU.* 18.2 (1990). 47-58.

Mbugua, Martin. "Ngugi's Life in Self Exile" and "Why I Advance African Langauges?" Nairobi: *Daily Nation's Weekender Magazine.* January 13, 1995.

Mbele, Joseph. "Language in African Literature: An Aside to Ngugi." *Research in African Literatures.* 23.1 (1992).

Monkman, Leslie. "Kenya and the New Jerusalem in *A Grain of Wheat.*" *African Literature Today.* 7 (1975). 111-16.

Muthali, Felix. "Continuity and Change in Conrad and Ngugi." *Kunapipi.* 2.1 (1981).

Narang, Harish. "Politics of Protest: Sub-Text in the Novels of Meja Wangi and Ngugi wa Thiong'o." *Mightier Than Matchet.* Ed. Harish Narang. New Delhi: Wiley Eastern, 1995.

Nazareth, Peter. *Literature and Society in Modern Africa.* Nairobi: East African Literature Bureau, 1972.

——. "The Second Home Coming: Multiple Ngugi's in *Petals of Blood.*" *Marxism and Literature.* Ed. George M. Gugelberger. Trenton: Africa World Press,1986.

Ngara, Emmanuel. *Stylistic Criticism and the African Novel.* London: Heinemann, 1982.

——. *Art, and Ideology in the African Novel.* London: Heinemann, 1985.

Nwonkwo, Chimalum. "Sifting and Grain from the Husk: An Overview of Ngugi's Writing." *The Literary Half-Yearly.* 25.1 (1984). 2-15.

Page, Malcom. "The Conclusions of Ngugi's *A Grain of Wheat*: Gloom or Affirmation?" *The Commonwealth in Canada.* Ed. Uma Maheswaran. Calcutta: Writers Workshop, 1983.

Palmer, Eustace. *An Introduction to the African Novel.* London: Heinemann, 1972.

——. "Petals of Blood." *The Growth of African Novel.* London: Heinemann, Pieterse, Cosmo, and Donald Munro, eds. *Protest and Conflict in African Literature.* London: Heinemann, 1969.

Peck, Richard. "Hermits and Saviours, Osagyefos and Healers: Artists and Intellectuals in the Works of Ngugi and Armah." *Research in African Literatures* 20.1 (1989). 26-49.

Pelsmakers, K. "A Hybrid Poetics in Ngugi's *Petals of Blood.*" *Commonwealth Novel in English.* 2.1 (1983). 7-26.

Petersen, Kirsten Holst. "Birth Pangs of a National

Consciousness: Mau Mau and Ngugi wa Thiong'o." *World Literature Written in English.* 20.2 (1981). 214-19.

Raj, Jagadish. "The Wounded Psyche of Africa as Reflected in Achebe's *Arrow of God,* Plomer's *Turbott Wolfe* and Ngugi's *The River Between.*" *Recent Commonwealth Literature.* Ed. R.K. Dhawan *et al.* New Delhi: Prestige Books, 1989.

Rao, Panduranga. "Ngugi A Grain of Wheat: A Resolution in the Hero Identification Confusion." *Recent Commonwealth Literature.* Ed. R.K. Dhawan, *et al.* New Delhi: Prestige Books, 1989.

Robson, Clifford B. *Ngugi wa Thiong'o.* London: Macmillan, 1979.

Sander, Reinhard. "Two Views of the Conflicts of Cultures in pre-Emergency Kenya." *The Literary Half-Yearly* 19.1 (1978).

Sharma, Govind N. "Ngugi's Detained as a Modern Consolation." *Research in African Literatures.* 196 (1988). 520-28.

——. "Ngugi's Apocalypse: Marxism, Christianity and African Utopianism in *Petals of Blood.*" *World Literature Written in English.* 18.2 (1979).

——. "Socialism and Civilization: The Revolutionary Traditionalism of Ngugi wa Thiong'o." *ARIEL.* 19.2 (1988).

Sicherman, Carol M. "Ngugi wa Thiong'o and the Writing of Kenyan History." *Research in African Literatures.* 20 (1989). 347-70.

Tinn, Christine M. "Music As a Point of Resistance in Ngugi wa Thiong'o's *Matigari.*" *UFAHAMU* 20.2 (1992). 2-17.

Verma, Charu. "Woman in Ngugi wa Thiong'o's Novels." *Mightier Than Matchet.* Ed. Harish Narang. New Delhi: Wiley Eastern, 1995.

Special Issues

Research in African Literatures: 26.2 (1985).

Africa Quarterly. Mightier Than Matcheat. 34.3 (1994).

Comparative Studies

Mathur, O.P. "The Hero Between: A Comparative Study of Ngugi's Waiyaki and Anand's Lalu," *Commonwealth Literature: Problems of Response*. Ed. Narasimhaiah C.D. Madras: Macmillan, 1978. 117-126.

Other Secondary Sources

Althusser, Louis. *Essays on Ideology*. London: Verso, 1984.

Amur, G.S. and S.K. Desai. Eds. *Colonial Consciousness in Commonwealth Literature*. Bombay: Somaiya, 1984.

Amur, G.S. and *et al.* Eds. *Indian Readings in Commonwealth Literature*. New Delhi: Sterling Publishers, 1985.

Asein, Samuel Omo and Albert Olu Ashaolu. *Studies in the African Novel*. Ibadan: Ibadan University Press, 1986.

Barnett, Donald L. and Karari Njama. *Mau Mau from Within*. London: MacGibben & Kee. n.d.

Beir, Ulili. 1967. *Introduction to African Literature*. London: Longman, 1973.

Booth, Wayne, C. *The Rhetoric of Fiction*. Chicago: University of Chicago, 1961.

Chinweizu. *The West and the Rest of Us: White Predators, Black Slaves and the African Elite*. Chicago: Vintage, 1990.

Cook, David. *African Literature: A Critical View*. London: Longman, 1977.

Dhawan, R.K. and *et al.* Eds. *Recent Commonwealth Literature*. 1 and 2, New Delhi: Prestige Books, 1989.

Eagleton, Terry. *Criticism and Ideology*. London: Verso, 1975.

——. 1983. *Literary Theory—An Introduction*. Oxford: Blackwell, 1985.

——. *Marxism and Literature: An Introduction*. London: Methuen. 1985.

Erikson, Erik H. *Childhood and Society*. 1950. New York: W.W. Norton, 1963.

Fanon, Frantz. 1961. *The Wretched of the Earth*. Trans. Constance Farrington, London: Penguin, 1990.

Fanon, Frantz. *Black Skin, White Masks.* Trans Charles Lam Markmann, London: Pluto Press, 1967.

Fast, Howard. 1950. *Literature and Reality.* Bombay: People's Publishing House, 1953.

Fischer, Ernest. *The Necessity of Art.* Harmondsworth: Penguin, 1959.

Forster, E.M. *Aspects of the Novel.* London: Arnold, 1927.

Gibaldi, Joseph and Walter S. Achtert. *MLA Hand Book For Writers of Research Papers.* III Edn. New Delhi: Wiley Eastern, 1989.

Gakwandi, Arthur S. *The Novel and Contemporary Experience in Africa.* London: Heinemann, 1977.

Gikandi, Simon. 1987. *Reading the African Novel.* London: James Currey and Heinemann, 1992.

Gregory, Robert G. *Quest for Equality: Asian Politics in East Africa 1900-1967.* New Delhi: Orient Longman, 1993.

——. *India and East Africa: A History of Race Relations within the British Empire, 1890-1939.* New Delhi: Orient Longman, 1972.

Harlow, Barbara. *Resistance Literature.* London: Methuen, 1987.

Harris, Joseph E. *Africans and their History.* 1972. New York: New American Library, 1987.

Heywood, C. Ed. *Perspectives on African Literature.* London: Heinemann, 1976.

Irele, Abiola. *The African Experience in Literature and Ideology.* London: Heinemann, 1981.

Iyengar, K.R. Srinivasa. *Indian Writing in English.* 1962. New Delhi: Sterling Publishers, 1995.

Jussawalla, Feroza and Reedway Dasenbrock. Eds. *Interviews with Writers of the Post-Colonial World.* Jackson, London: University Press of Mississippi, 1992.

Kenyatta, Jomo. *Facing Mount Kenya.* 1938. Nairobi: East African Educational Publications, 1992.

Kumar, Shiv K. Ed. *Critical Approaches to Fiction.* New York: McGraw Hill, 1968.

Larson, Charles R. *The Emergence of African Fiction.* 1971. London: Macmillan, 1978.

Lechte, John. *Fifty Contemporary Thinkers from Structuralism to Post-Modernity.* London: Rouledge, 1994.

Lindsforth, Bernth. "East is East and West is West: Points of Divergence in African Literary History." *Awakened Conscience.* Ed. C.D. Narasimhaiah. New Delhi: Sterling Publishers, 1978.

Lubbock, Percy. *The Craft of Fiction.* New York: Charles Scribner's Sons, 1921.

Mannoni, O. *Prospero and Caliban.* 1950. Trans. Pamela Powerland. London: Mcthuen, 1956.

Memmi, Albert. *The Colonizer and the Colonized.* New York: The Orion Press, 1965.

Moore, Gerald. *Twelve African Writers.* 1980. London: Heinemann, 1983.

Mukherjee, Arun P. "Whose Post-Colonialism and Whose Post-Modernism?" *World Literature Written in English.* 3.2 (1990).

Mukherjee, Meenakshi. *The Twice Born Fiction: Themes and Techniques of the Indian Novel in English.* 1971. New Delhi: Arnold-Heinemann, 1974.

Nadel, George and Perry Curtis. Eds. *Imperialism and Colonialism.* 1964. Toronto: Macmillan, 1968.

Nandy, Ashis. *The Intimate Enemy: The Loss and Recovery of Self Under Colonialism.* Delhi: Oxford University Press, 1983.

Naik, M.K. Ed. *Aspects of Indian Writing in English.* Madras: Macmillan, 1992.

Naik, M.K. *et al.* Eds. *Critical Essays on Indian Writing in English.* 1968. Madras: Macmillan, 1977.

Ngara, Emmanuel. *Stylistic Criticism and the African Novel.* London: Heinemann, 1982.

Narang, Harish. Ed. *Mightier Than Matchet.* New Delhi: Wiley Eastern Ltd., 1995.

Narasimhaiah, C.D. Ed. *Awakened Conscience: Studies in Commonwealth Literature.* Madras: Macmillan, 1978.

——. Ed. *Commonwealth Literature: Problems of Response.* Madras: Macmillan, 1981.

Nazareth, Peter. *Literature and Society in Modern Africa.* Nairobi: East African Literature Bureau, 1972.

Nkumah, Kwame. *Neo-Colonialism: The Last Stage of Imperialism.* London: Heinemann Educational Book, 1965.

Odinga, Oginga. *Not Yet Uhuru.* London: Heinemann, 1967.

Palmer, Eustace. *An Introduction to the African Novel.* London: Heinemann, 1972.

p'Betek, Okot. *Africa's Cultural Revolution.* Nairobi: Macmillan, 1973.

Pieterse, Cosmo and Donald Munro. Eds. *Protest and Conflict in African Literature.* London: Heinemann, 1969.

Said, Edward W. *Culture and Imperialism.* London: Chatto & Windus, 1993.

Srivastava, Ramesh K. Ed. *Colonial Consciousness in Black American, African and Indian Fiction in English.* Jalandhar: ABS Publications, 1991.

Viramani, K.K. "Marks of India in Swahili Culture." *Africa Quarterly.* 22.1 (Indian Council For Cultural Relations, New Delhi). n.d.

Walsh, William. Ed. *Readings in Commonwealth Literature.* London: Oxford University Press, 1973.

Williams, Patric and Laura Chrisman. eds. *Colonial Discourse and Post-Colonial Theory: A Reader.* New York: Harester Wheatsheaf, 1993.

Williams, Raymond. *Marxism and Literature.* Oxford: Oxford University Press, 1977.